INSTITUTIONAL TRIGGERING

A Guide to Take CLTS to Scale

KAMAL KAR

INDIA • SINGAPORE • MALAYSIA

ISBN

Hardcase 979-8-89724-935-0
Paperback 979-8-89026-474-9

Contents

Summary 7

Key Definitions 9

Foreword 13

About the Book 17

Abbreviations 21

Acknowledgements 25

Chapter 1 Introduction to Institutional Triggering 31

The Background and Context 32

What is CLTS? 32

What Has Happened Since the Introduction of CLTS over the Years? 35

What is Institutional Triggering? 42

The Need for Institutional Triggering 46

Typology of Institutional Triggering 51

Institutional Triggering at Different Levels of Government Institutions Compared 53

Phases of Institutional Triggering in CLTS 62

Challenges of Scaling up of CLTS Approach Those Can be Addressed by Institutional Triggering 63

1. Inadequate or Partial Understanding of CLTS Amongst Senior Decision-Makers 64
2. Weak Policy Context 70

3. Absence of Innovative Funding Mechanisms............. 72
4. Institutional Open Defecation..................................... 73
5. Humanitarian Conflict and Emergency Context....... 78
6. WASH and Climate Change... 82
7. Weak or Unclear Strategy for Taking CLTS to Scale...... 84
8. Poor Inter-Institutional Coordination........................ 86
Key Issues and Context for Institutional Triggering....... 88

Chapter 2 Institutional Triggering Methodology.........................93

Who Are the Participants for Institutional Triggering?......98
Who Should Facilitate Institutional Triggering? 99
Duration of the Institutional Triggering Process 102
Institutional Triggering at Different Levels.................... 103

National Level 103
SubNational/Regional Level...................................... 106
District Level 109

A. Stage 1: Institutional Pre-Triggering........................ 110

Steps to follow during Institutional Pre-Triggering.. 114

B. Stage 2: Institutional Triggering................................ 119

Steps in the Triggering Process................................. 120
Phase A of Institutional Triggering: Tools and Sequence of Application 121
Precautions for Institutional Triggering 133
Phase B of Institutional Triggering: Targets and Roadmap... 144

C. Stage 3: Institutional Post-Triggering Follow-Up..... 163

Inter Institutional Review Committee 165

Chapter 3 Impact Monitoring of Institutional Triggering.........169

How to Monitor the Impact of Institutional Triggering........171

At the National Level........171

At the Subnational Level........173

At the Individual Level........175

Community and Institutional Triggering Compared.....176

Chapter 4 Recognizing Success........196

Instant Ignition of National Spirit: Best Outcome........197

Convinced, Yet Confused!........206

How to Begin: Who Will Bell the Cat?........209

References........219

About the Author........223

Summary

Institutional Triggering is a proven methodology for convincing senior-level decision-makers and WASH sector leaders about the strength and efficacy of the Community Led Total Sanitation (CLTS) approach. It also helps in breaking the traditional perspectives and myths regarding unwillingness, inability or lack of initiative of the poor to improve their own sanitation situation and liberate themselves from the drudgery and pangs of life through self-mobilization. If applied systematically, successful institutional triggering facilitates the process of enhancing the much-needed sanitation policy change at the national level which fast-tracks the spread and scaling-up of CLTS towards attaining the status of a respectable nation. There are many examples of systematic efforts to trigger high-level decision-makers those resulted in faster sanitation coverage through the scaling-up of CLTS.

There are unique examples of community led collective initiatives in countries those exist in isolation. These powerful examples are often brushed under the carpet of large-scale government-led, subsidised hardware centric sanitation programmes which hardly results in any tangible positive health outcomes. Often, in places where all households of a community were saturated with toilets constructed by governments or NGOs, hardly any reduction in the practice of OD was noticed. In other words, the newly constructed toilets were used for all purposes other than the purpose for which they were built. Since the most important element of collective behaviour change was missing in the traditional subsidized approach of sanitation, it often resulted in very low usage of toilets.

Institutional triggering is largely used to bring on board the institutions and organisations responsible for improving sanitation and show them the way to empower local communities in a rational and convincing way. Often, middle- and junior-level officials of the government and other establishment are not too keen to change the status quo and move out of their comfort zones by changing the old practice of top-down instruction and free distribution of sanitary hardware materials or money. In general, there had been resistance to welcome and adopt any new approach that might create pressure on the existing workload and demanded innovative thinking. This is particularly common among older officers approaching retirement or superannuation, who generally have limited flexibility to adopt new ideas. Dishonesty, lack of transparency and a nexus between contractors and technical officials including fear of losing control, and issuance of top-down directives, etc., could sometimes be the determining factors. Attitudes of elitism and pride in possessing university degrees and higher qualifications often become barriers to the smooth scaling-up of CLTS due to the superiority complex of some officials who consider the end users as beneficiary and inferior human beings. Additionally, complex paraphernalia and top down practice of implementing large scale programmes of the government rigidly linked with sanction, orders and directives sometimes hamper the flexibility and promptness essential for decision-making based on the emerging local needs.

Key Definitions

CLTS	Community-Led Total Sanitation (CLTS) is an innovative approach for empowering communities to completely eliminate open defecation (OD) and to begin the journey towards a sustained improvement in public health. It focuses on igniting a change in collective hygiene behaviour, which is achieved through a process of collective local action stimulated by facilitators from within or outside the community. CLTS is an outcome-focused approach involving no hardware subsidy, and it does not prescribe latrine models at the outset.
Champions	Champions are those who contribute substantially in carrying forward the CLTS/ safe sanitation campaign at the community, district, region or at the national level. They can contribute in any form such as by 1. sparing their time 2. Finances wherever required 3. Organising group meetings 4. Advocacy with the elders and other important people 5. Coordinating between the institutions and the community 6. Highlighting and campaigning the success of local communities

Community Consultants	Community consultants drawn from among the most successful and motivated natural leaders who have already gained experience actively supporting the achievement of ODF status in their own communities and who are capable of doing the same in neighbouring and/or distant communities. Such expertise is being systematically drawn to trigger CLTS and provide follow-up to other communities in the district or state within the country by the government and other international organisations.
CRAP	The CLTS Rapid Appraisal Protocol is a diagnostic tool to assess the status and quality of CLTS programming in a country by reviewing the present practice of CLTS at the national, sub-national (regional or district), and community levels by involving a diverse range of stakeholders at each level.
Institutional Triggering	This is a methodology developed to trigger institutional actors to take ownership and responsibility for the state of poor sanitation in the country/state/region and mobilise immediate action to support the implementation and scaling up of CLTS in the respective area.
Natural Leaders	Natural leaders are enthusiasts who emerge and can be empowered to take on a leadership role to transform their own community to become ODF. Natural leaders help in motivating their fellow community members, in monitoring the progress as households become ODF and to ensure that the collective behaviour change is sustained. These natural leaders may emerge from any section of the society, e.g., young, elderly, men, women, children, etc.

ODF	Open Defecation Free is a status when the entire community moves from OD to the practice of safe sanitation by using or sharing latrines. Therefore no faeces, including children's poo, are exposed to the open air in the surrounding areas. An ODF village is one where: • *There is no shit outside and everybody uses a latrine* • *The latrine's pit and platform are clean, covered and fly proof* • *Handwashing facilities are available next to all the latrines and everyone washes hands with clean water, and soap.*
ODF Celebration	This is an event when the achievement of ODF status by a community is verified, acknowledged, and felicitated officially by the relevant authorities (e.g., local government, district, region, state, etc.) involving formal and informal leaders of the area.
ODF Learning Laboratory	Successful and unique examples of ODF villages are showcased as models or learning laboratories for sharing the best practices with other communities in the area or region. Such spontaneous and informal dissemination of locally developed best practices is very useful as a scaling-up strategy.
ODF Verification	This is a formal system for verifying and validating the ODF claims of a community and the process by which a community gets certified as ODF by a third-party or independent and unbiased outside agency.
Triggering – Community	This is a process of mobilising people in a community to visually analyse their sanitation situation and adverse effects of OD through a series of participatory exercises, with the aim of motivating them to stop the practise of OD and take collective action towards becoming open defecation free (ODF).

Foreword

As a form of collective action, community-led total sanitation (CLTS) has proven highly effective. It has empowered communities to end the practice of open defecation, invest their own resources in sanitation improvements, and adopt safe hygiene behaviors. Since its inception in Bangladesh twenty-five years ago, the application of CLTS has empowered over 200 million people to pursue sanitation solutions throughout Africa, Asia, and Latin America.

Households in the local communities that act collectively to improve sanitation in their communities derive immediate dividends. They enjoy better health outcomes and improved school attendance, resulting in enhanced capacity and productivity in agriculture, industry, and services. They also achieve a high degree of self-dignity, trust among households, and the realisation that by taking steps to improve their sanitation, they have the power to participate in decision-making processes that affect their lives. As active partners, rather than passive recipients, in sustainable development, they engage government and NGOs to create solutions to improve security, education, and healthcare, among other related basic services.

In its most successful applications, CLTS has produced cadres of "natural leaders" who, having facilitated open-defecation-free conditions in their respective communities, work with their counterparts in other localities to mobilise entire wards and districts, in some instances assuming leadership roles in local government.

This publication is a welcome addition to the literature as it brings attention to the fact that much of the success of CLTS has come about not only through local community action but also through institutional triggering. That is, the application of CLTS methods to bring about changes in the behaviour of policy makers and practitioners about how to enable community action to improve sanitation at scale.

One should not underestimate the need for institutional triggers. Since its inception, practitioners of CLTS have faced formidable resistance from subnational, national, and international institutions, in what the author of this publication provocatively called "institutional open defecation".

Among the most pervasive forms of resistance is the deployment of household sanitation hardware subsidies for the construction of toilets. Sanitation subsidies perpetuate a culture of dependency. They fail to end the practice of open defecation and do little to instill good hygiene, be it handwashing practices or the maintenance of toilets. Further, the disbursement of sanitation subsidies is particularly vulnerable to ownership, repair, and maintenance, and often corruption.

By targeting policy makers in structured interventions, institutional triggering raises awareness about the negative implications of open defecation, the inadequacies of subsidies, and the effectiveness of approaches based upon community empowerment and sustained behaviour change. Institutional triggering has been applied across geographies and in diverse institutional settings, from local councils to national assemblies, among Cabinet ministers and heads of state.

Institutional triggering is also effective in addressing another form of institutional open defecation, namely tensions between and within Ministries of Health, Ministries of Water, Ministries of Public Work, etc. Targeted interventions based on CLTS principles help governments establish institutional arrangements that assign responsibilities for sanitation, often with one ministry providing overall policy coherence and the other providing operational support. They can also involve ministries of education, finance, and women's affairs so that sanitation programming is integrated across sectors, effectively utilising public expenditure.

Even when governments agree on the division of labour, the ministries of health tend to privilege cure over prevention, and the ministries of water prioritise water supply to the exclusion of sanitation. Flexible in its application, institutional triggering helps make the case for ministries of health to invest in prevention and for ministries of water to integrate sanitation, water supply, and water resource management.

Applications of institutional triggering help to ensure that sanitation solutions promote, rather than undermining, equality and discrimination. Generic toilet designs may address the needs of some parts of the population but not others. Persons experiencing limited mobility, including children, menstruating women, the elderly, and pregnant women, require sanitation solutions that meet their needs at home, in school, and at the workplace. By orienting discussions among policymakers and by promoting the voice of agency of women, youth, and the differently abled, institutional triggering can at once address sanitation needs comprehensively and reduce forms of exclusion and discrimination.

National and local governments do not operate in a vacuum. Their policies, budgeting, and programming on sanitation are linked to the strategic priorities of international institutions that are often incoherent, constituting yet another form of institutional open defecation.

In March 2023, the United Nations General Assembly, for the first time since 1977, convened the Water Conference to advance the water action agenda. The conference was effective in elevating Sustainable Development Goal 6 on Water and Sanitation, among the 17 Goals of the 2030 Agenda on Sustainable Development, and in urging Member States to make water a crucial component of climate action, energy, health, urban development, and disaster risk reduction, as well as peace and security.

While helpful in putting water back on the global agenda, the Water Conference was less than successful in promoting sanitation and hygiene. As is the case with World Water Week, the World Water Forum, and World Water Day, the Water Conference provided only limited attention to sanitation. Lost was the opportunity to provide policy coherence on

CLTS, prevention, and integrated approaches to water supply, sanitation, and hygiene.

It will be important moving forward for the protagonist of CLTS to take institutional triggering to the international level. This will involve drawing upon the success of triggering at the community, subnational, and national levels captured in this publication. And applying these to international finance institutions, multilateral agencies, and bilateral development cooperation agencies, as well as the machinery of international NGOs and consulting firms contracted to execute water and sanitation programmes.

Christopher W. Williams,

Director of the New York Office of the United Nations Human Settlements Programme, UN-Habitat, and the former Executive Director of the Water Supply and Sanitation Collaborative Council.

About the Book

It has been about 21 years since the inception of Community-Led Total Sanitation (CLTS) and the introduction of the methodology within the larger framework of sanitation globally. For the first time, the term 'ODF' (Open Defecation Free) was incorporated in the vocabulary of Water Sanitation and Hygiene (WASH) policies and programmes wherever access to safe sanitation was either lacking or proper hygiene behaviour was not practiced. CLTS witnessed a rapid spread and covered more than 73 countries, benefiting an ever-increasing number of villages, communes, subdistricts, districts, and regions. Moreover, the traditional method of providing subsidised or free sanitation hardware coupled with top-down teaching of hygiene education to communities began to fade away. In many countries, self-mobilised communities began to construct toilets of various location-specific appropriate models by mobilising their own resources. This movement began with the realisation that open defecation can contaminate the food chain and affect anyone in a village, even if the household possesses a safe sanitary toilet. If one person defecates in the open, everybody in the community could be in danger of ingesting the dangerous faecal contaminant spreading through different pathways like hooves of grazing animals, shoes of pedestrians, bicycles, rainwater, flies, winds, etc. It was also realised that washing hands with soap at critical times was of paramount importance for the health of people, especially children.

In order to fully realise the benefits of CLTS, a much larger and more influential group of stakeholders outside the triggered communities is required to be engaged in the dialogue and be triggered to enable and facilitate large-scale improvements in the sanitation sector and policy. Important stakeholders in sanitation included senior decision-makers of governments, international and national institutions, government ministries, federal and district administration, academia, private sector executives, leaders of NGOs, religious organisations, civil society, and donors.

This book explains the need for Institutional Triggering (IT) as an important tool to complement the CLTS methodology and influence institutional actors, policy and decision-makers within government ministries to scale up their homegrown success of CLTS across the nation. It describes how facilitators are supposed to engage and interact with high officials and senior leaders and convince them to be proactive and act to multiply the success of CLTS in regions where access to safe sanitation is poor or non-existent.

While the book emphasises that there is no rigidity in the methodology for triggering, it does broadly elaborate an applicable framework for triggering institutions flexibly. The central goal of institutional triggering is to ensure that positive outcomes are achieved on a larger scale by triggering institutions and making them aware of CLTS and its power to ensure safe sanitation, thereby enhancing prosperity. Through careful analyses of multiple case studies of institutional triggering from countries in Asia, Africa, and Latin America, the book highlights the challenges and concerns of influencing sanitation policy for an achievable strategic rollout plan. The case studies also highlight how the institutional triggering methodology is tailored to influence different levels of leadership in different country contexts.

In order to achieve SDG target 6.2 (ending the practice of open defecation globally) by 2030, it is crucial to demonstrate the power of local communities to improve their own sanitation situation by themselves. If committed, the senior decisionmakers could influence and change the national sanitation policies focused more on community empowerment.

The consequences of the absence of the right enabling environment and a robust sanitation policy could be reflected in many ways, like poor public health, a weak workforce, children with slow cognitive development, poor performances in school, etc., eventually slowing down the GDP of a nation.

This book will be useful in guiding a variety of users, ranging from government ministers and high-level executives all the way down to local and district administrators responsible for the overall development. It also attempts to unpack the importance of an appropriate and enabling environment for the spread and success of CLTS and the dire need to imbibe the principles of local empowerment in the policies and strategies of respective institutions. The book provides a robust framework and a complete roadmap to follow as a guideline towards establishing an ODF nation, ultimately achieving the SDG 6.2 by 2030.

Abbreviations

CC	Community Consultant
CBO	Community based Organisation
CDO	Chief Development Officer
CM	Chief Minister
CMR	Child Mortality Rate
CRAP	CLTS Rapid Appraisal Protocol
CSO	Civil Society Organisation
CLTS	Community-Led Total Sanitation
DCD	District Coordinating Director
DCE	District Coordinating Executive
DEHO	District Environmental Health Officer
DFID	Department of International Development, UK
DRM	Deputy Regional Minister
ELC	Experiential Learning Cycle
ESARO	Eastern and Southern Africa Regional Office of UNICEF
FAA	Fonds d' Appuipourl' Assainissement/Global Sanitation Fund in Madagascar
GDP	Gross Domestic Product
GP	Gram Panchayat

GSF	Global Sanitation Fund
HDI	Human Development Index
IDP	Internally Displaced People
IDS	Institute of Development Studies
INGO	International Non-Governmental Organizations
IT	Institutional Triggering
MDCSS	Ministry of Community Development and Social Services
MLGH	Ministry of Local Government and Housing,
MLGRD	Ministry of Local Government and Rural Development
MMR	Maternal Mortality Rate
MOE	Ministry of Education
MOH	Ministry of Health
MOHA	Ministry of Home Affairs
MOIB	Ministry of Information and Broadcasting
MOU	Memorandum of Understanding
NBA	Nirmal Bharat Abhiyan
NESSAP	National Environmental Sanitation Strategy Action Plan, Ghana & IRC
NGO	Non-Governmental Organizations
NL	Natural Leader
OD	Open Defecation
ODF	Open Defecation Free

PHAST	Participatory Hygiene and Sanitation Transformation.
SARAR	Self-Esteem, Associative Strengths, Resourcefulness, Action-Planning and Responsibility
SBM	Swachh Bharat Mission
SGD	Sustainable Development Goal
SLWM	Solid and Liquid Waste Management
SMART	Specific, Measurable, Achievable, Realistic, and Time-bound
TSC	Total Sanitation Campaign
U5MR	Under-5 Mortality Rate
VIP	Ventilated Improved Pit
WASH	Water, Sanitation, and Hygiene
WCARO	Western and Central Africa Regional Office of UNICEF
WESLIC	Water and Sanitation for Low Income Communities Project, Indonesia
WHO	World Health Organisation
WSSCC	Water Supply and Sanitation Collaborative Council

Acknowledgements

This publication draws strongly in parts from the original *Handbook on Community-Led Total Sanitation* by Kamal Kar with Robert Chambers, published by Plan International (UK) in 2008, and 'From Village to Nation Scaling-Up Community-Led Total Sanitation', by Kamal Kar, 2019, by Practical Action, UK. Thanks are due to all those who contributed to the development of the original document.

A good deal of change and modification has taken place in the methodology, applications, scaling-up, and institutionalisation of CLTS across the globe, and many new lessons have emerged. I must apologise that it has taken me so long to produce a coherent and comprehensive update in the form of the book presented here, which is long overdue. This book, *Institutional Triggering: A Guide to Take CLTS to Scale,* has been developed by drawing on the experiences of many individuals and organisations in many countries in Asia, Africa, Latin America and the Pacific. While it is not easy to thank all of them individually, I must put on record the contributions of the following persons and organisations.

I would like to thank Dr. Christopher W. Williams, Director of the New York Office of the United Nations Human Settlements Programme, UN-Habitat, and the former Executive Director of the Water Supply and Sanitation Collaborative Council, for writing the foreword for the book.

My sincere thanks to Ms. Ann Thomas, Senior WASH Advisor, UNICEF New York, for taking the time to review the manuscript and give her valuable suggestions. She has also written a message for the book.

I would also like to thank Prof. Robert Chambers for encouraging me all through the process of writing the book and for emphasising the need for the book to trigger institutions to ensure a wider local empowerment towards ending the practice of open defecation.

My thanks are also due to the WASH Programme countries under ESARO (Nairobi) and WCARO (Dakar). I would especially like to thank the heads of WASH programmes and Country Representatives of UNICEF in Eretria, Sudan, Ethiopia, Somalia, Uganda, Kenya, Malawi, Mozambique, Zambia, Lesotho, Swaziland, and Namibia of ESARO, and Ghana, Nigeria, Chad, Mali, Sierra Leone, Liberia, Benin, Ivory Coast, Senegal, Niger, Burkina Faso, and Mauritania of WCARO. I would also like to mention the following people, who have contributed in different ways, either by sharing experiences or data at different stages of writing this book: Dr. Shyamal Shah's (a consultant and associate of the CLTS Foundation) contribution at different stages in writing the book is appreciated.

I would like to thank Yirgalem Solomon of UNICEF Eritrea for her contribution in documenting the experience of an institutional triggering event held in Eritrea.

I would like to sincerely thank Ms. Nuzhat Shahzadi of UNICEF, who was the country team leader in Kiribati in the Pacific and was instrumental in inviting me to the island nation to introduce CLTS. Nuzhat led the scaling up of the CLTS campaign with her colleagues and government ministry officials. She has illustrated the timeline of introduction, spread, and institutionalisation of CLTS in Kiribati in the relevant section of this book. She has further explained how the governmental policy underwent a change from an individual household subsidy approach to a no-subsidy CLTS approach for local empowerment.

I am grateful to Alex Grumbley of WaterAid Timor-Leste, Heather Moran of the BESIK programme supported by DFAT, the Government of Australia, Sr. Elias Pereira, Secretary of State for Water, Sanitation, and Urbanisation in Timor-Leste, and Senor Domingos, Governor of Bobonaro District, for their contributions in the process of institutionalising CLTS in Timor-Leste. Alex, Heather, Sr. Pereira, and Sr. Domingos worked tirelessly to sustain the campaign for open defecation-free Timor-Leste. By involving all the major actors in sanitation in the country through consistent and functional involvement, they sustained the process of grounding CLTS by influencing government policies.

I would like to register my sincere thanks to Leonard Mukosha of the Ministry of Health, Government of Zambia, for his contribution in sharing the unique mechanism of scaling up CLTS through the involvement of the Traditional Chiefs of Zambia. Zambia has 288 Chiefdoms, of which more than 40 have already achieved ODF status, mainly through the active involvement of the local traditional leaders under the guidance of chiefs in the scaling-up of the process.

I would like to express my heartfelt thanks to the village chiefs and local and natural leaders of thousands of communities across the world for sharing their perspectives on ways of bridging the gap between the outside agencies and the communities.

I would also like to thank H.E. Chreay Pom of the Ministry of Rural Development, Government of Cambodia, for his efforts in the institutionalisation of CLTS in Cambodia. My thanks are also due to the Provincial Governors and Deputy Governors of the provinces of Pursat, Kampong Chhnang, Siem Reap, Kampong Cham, Preah Vihear, Ratanakiri, and Kampong Thom. I would like to especially mention the involvement of H.E Kith Sopha Deputy Governor of Pursat Province, who made a powerful speech to inspire all the Deputy Governors at a national conference on the need for the institutionalisation of CLTS.

I would like to profusely thank Dr. Kefa Ombacho, Chief Public Health Officer of the Ministry of Health, Government of Kenya, for his powerful contribution to institutionalising the approach in government policy and rolling it out across the country. With Dr. Ombacho's initiative, CLTS was adopted as an approach in the country's WASH planning.

Dr. Ombacho was one of the early champions of CLTS and was instrumental not only in institutionalising the approach within Kenya but also in influencing the national sanitation policies of many other Anglophone African nations in the region. Learning from the example of Kenya, the leaders from the neighbouring countries realised the dire need and urgency for transforming the collective hygiene behaviour of the rural and urban populations to improve the efficiency of primary health.

I would also like to thank Mr. Solomon Kebede, Oliver, and Theresa McDonnell from Vita for their roles and efforts in institutionalising the CLTS approach in the countrywide programme of Vita, Ethiopia, in the early ages. Mr. John Weakliam, CEO of Vita in Dublin, Ireland, took the initiative in pulling the thread of strong community participation from a large number of ODF villages in the Arba Minch area of Ethiopia and supported the CLTS Foundation in designing the Community-Led Total Stove programme. The CLT-Stove programme was aimed at saturating the villages with improved cookstoves by totally eliminating sost gulicha or three-stone traditional cooking to reduce rapid and uncontrolled destruction of vegetation and other natural sources as fuel. The CLT-Stove programme has been gaining momentum in the Gamo zone of Ethiopia.

I am thankful to all my colleagues and consultants at the CLTS Foundation, especially Preetha Prabhakaran, Tathabrata Bhattacharya, Megha Sen, Aparupa Dutta, and Katherine Pasteur, for their help and support at different times in the course of writing this book.

Without the help and active support of Mrs. Swati Kar, my wife, it would not have been possible for me to write this book, which already took years to complete. Her support has been extremely valuable at times when the demand for my time was very high for assignments to many countries related to development of livelihood and WASH programmes.

I would like to put on record the contributions, help and support of Ms. Priyanka Jaiswal, Programme Officer, CLTS Foundation Global that have been remarkable.

I hope that this book will be useful in instilling the value of community participation in national sanitation policies alongside the development of sanitation infrastructure by the governments of many countries.

Unfortunately, the doubt on the community's role and capability of transforming the sanitation scenario is amply reflected in the opinions of some senior WASH officials of the government and the UN. 'Governments are not willing to make seismic changes to the enabling environment for CLTS alone'. The priority is still largely focused on top-down hardware infrastructure investment, undermining the community's role in decision-making, mobilisation of local resources, and participation as an active partner in development. Although this scenario is changing in many countries, it has to go a long way if we are to achieve SDG 6.2 by 2030.

His Excellency Mr Hery Rajaonarimampianina, President of the Republic of Madagascar, signs a pledge to end open defecation in Madagascar in March, 2015

Chapter 1

Introduction to Institutional Triggering

THE BACKGROUND AND CONTEXT

It has been two decades since community-led total sanitation (CLTS) emerged as an approach to eliminating open defecation (OD). Its introduction and spread to various countries across the developing world led to increased access to sanitation for millions of people[1]. While the CLTS methodology demonstrated quick results in achieving open defecation-free (ODF) communities, scaling up this approach with quality emerged as a key challenge in most countries. Lack of an enabling environment appeared to be one of the most important challenges for scaling up CLTS in many countries. National and local governments, along with NGOs and development partners, have taken various steps to address this challenge, resulting in the emergence of many innovative scaling-up mechanisms around the globe. Over the years, the CLTS Foundation has worked with many national governments and their local partners to systematically institutionalise CLTS and scale up the approach for nationwide coverage. One of the most important challenges was to bring different institutions, ministries, and departments together on a common platform to fight the overarching issue of poor sanitation that affected everyone across the nation. This book captures many such experiences and provides a step-by-step guide on the methodology of *Institutional Triggering.*

WHAT IS CLTS?

CLTS is an innovative approach for empowering communities to eliminate OD and climb the sanitation ladder by improving their sanitation practices, thereby ensuring positive health and environmental outcomes. It focuses on igniting a change in the collective sanitation and hygiene behaviour of a community, which is achieved through a

1 Kamal Kar and Robert Chambers, *Handbook on Community-Led Total Sanitation.* Plan UK, 2008 and Venkataramanan, Vidya, et al. "Community-Led Total Sanitation: A Mixed-Methods Systematic Review of Evidence and Its Quality." *Environmental Health Perspectives,* vol. 126, no. 2, 2018, doi:10.1289/ehp1965.

process of participatory communal analysis of their own sanitation practices. This is followed by collective local action stimulated by the facilitators from within or outside the community (Kar, 2008). The CLTS process emphasises the shared benefit of stopping OD rather than focusing on individual hygiene behaviour change or building toilets alone as a solution. Stopping the practice of OD by the entire community always encourages collective local actions and strengthens local cooperation. In this context, the community decides how to create a clean and hygienic environment that benefits everyone by liberating them from the risk and danger of ingesting each other's faeces spread through the practise of OD. It is also crucial that no upfront household subsidy on sanitation hardware or top-down prescriptions of models be provided (Kar, 2008).

A combination of powerful triggering tools and methods and its simplicity have enabled the CLTS approach to transcend political, linguistic, cultural, ethnic, and religious boundaries in order to achieve its purpose. The methodology for community triggering has been refined over many years of practice and experience in over 73 countries globally. It is well documented in the publications, '*Scaling Up CLTS From Village to Nation*', '*Handbook on Community-Led Total Sanitation*', and '*Facilitating "Hands-On" Training Workshops for Community-Led Total Sanitation. A Trainers' Training Guide*', *written by Dr. Kamal Kar* (Kar 2019; Kar, 2008; Kar, 2010 respectively), the pioneer of the approach. The facilitation process is divided into four key stages, each of which is equally important:

- Pre-triggering: Entry point preparation and activities to enter the community
- Triggering: Mobilising the community through the ignition of CLTS
- Post-triggering follow-up: Ensuring collective community action
- Post-ODF activities: Sustaining community behaviour change and scaling up

Apart from the above four activities at the community level, it is very important to continue a host of institutional follow-up activities for sustainability. As mentioned earlier, the primary objective of institutional triggering is to stimulate the institutions responsible for maintaining safe sanitation at various levels of a country or region. As the roles of institutions differ from the district through the region to the national level, the focus, design and content of the training on institutional triggering should address the real needs of the participants. While the participants at the district level and below need to learn more about the skills and methodology of triggering, the players at the national level should acquire sound knowledge and understanding as to how a right sanitation policy would ensure stronger local participation. It is difficult to imagine a participatory bottom-up approach in organisations those are governed and administered in a traditionally top-down mode. It is, therefore, not very easy to institutionalise a participatory CLTS approach within an institution that is attuned to working in a hierarchical directive mode.

While CLTS facilitation involves no prescription and rigidity, it does utilise a set of participatory tools to 'trigger' community members into collective local action through their own realisation of ingesting one another's faeces through the practice of OD (Kar, 2008). The triggering tools include community mapping of open defecation areas; transect walks through the village; calculating the amount and volume of faeces produced everyday and over a period of time by the entire community; major diseases and illnesses caused by poor sanitation; calculating medical expenses; and analysing faecal-oral transmission routes (Kar, 2008). The triggering or ignition moment is characterised by some members of the community experiencing strong emotions of disgust and shame, which transpire into motivation for collective behaviour change and ending the practise of OD. Upon realising the consequences of ingesting faecal matter, the natural leaders and proactive members mobilise the entire community to develop a plan of action, change its hygiene behaviour, and stop the practice of OD. Unhygienic practices by any one member of the community perpetuate the cycle of faecal contamination in the food chain and its various negative impacts. The collective desire to achieve a totally ODF environment becomes very pronounced through self-help, social solidarity, sharing of resources and expertise, and other forms of collective action. It all begins with stopping the practice of OD first, followed by handwashing with soap or ash at critical times (after defecation and before handling food), and then moving on to other hygienic behaviour practices and improvements in the latrine and other sanitation facilities.

In most places, a successful ODF community does not stop their collective local action by ending the practice of open defecation alone. In fact, the empowered ODF community moves on to tackle other social and behavioural problems like large-scale absenteeism of teachers and students from school, ending seasonal hunger for some families due to non-availability of food, cash, work in the area, forcing compulsory seasonal migration, large-scale exploitation of the poor by the loan sharks, alcoholism, domestic violence, etc.

WHAT HAS HAPPENED SINCE THE INTRODUCTION OF CLTS OVER THE YEARS?

The CLTS approach was developed in 2000 in Bangladesh and spread across 70 countries within the next 10 years. However, it took more time for the approach to be adopted and incorporated into the national sanitation policies of the countries where the traditional subsidised or free hardware supply-driven sanitation approach was being rolled out by the governments being supported by bilateral, multilateral, or international non-governmental organisations (INGOs). Basically, the principle of local empowerment and handing over the stick to the local communities was not truly adopted in the national sanitation policies. CLTS approach got diluted at the level of implementation wherever it was adopted on a ad-hoc basis but not incorporated into the national sanitation policy. As a result, the same old practice of a top-down, prescriptive hardware supply-driven sanitation approach continued as before. However, it took a lot of time initially to scale up CLTS from a few ODF villages to entirely open-defecation-free districts, regions, and nations. Interestingly, there was a huge variation in the time for scaling up CLTS in different countries. In countries where there was no provision for hardware sanitation subsidies at the household level, the progress of adoption and scaling up of the community-led approach was much faster than in countries where it was supply-driven by external agencies. In areas where a supply-driven sanitation approach was followed, the level of ownership, proper usage of facilities, and household investment for repair and maintenance by the recipient families were pathetic. Families did not understand the need for safe sanitation facilities but continued the age-old practice of open defecation. It took time for CLTS to find a place in the national sanitation policies of many nations. One of the most important reasons for the delay in the adoption of the community-led approach in the national sanitation policy of some country was mainly due to availability of free funding and grants for construction of free toilets by the external donor agencies. This was attractive and easy for the government of many countries who were sold to the donor agencies idea of attaching more importance to sanitation hardware before behaviour change. As a result, hundreds of thousands of toilets were built, most of which remained un-utilised or underutilised while OD continued. Organisations supporting the development of women and children, among others, spent huge amounts of money to these countries to improve their sanitation facilities. For example, Participatory Hygiene and Sanitation Transformation (PHAST) or Self-esteem, Associative Strengths, Resourcefulness, Action-Planning, and Responsibility (SARAR) were being funded by external donors agencies those came along with the instruction of how to distribute the grant to the beneficiaries. Most countries could not afford to refuse the donation or grant that came with a prescription of approach and methodology for implementation from outside.

Although the national policymakers and senior planners of some countries were convinced about the efficacy of the CLTS approach, they could not adopt it by replacing the earlier policy, mainly because of many limitations beyond their control. Most of these countries entered into bilateral agreements with external funding agencies to follow a traditional, subsidised approach to sanitation. Therefore, they had no choice but to continue with the old approach and provide subsidised or free sanitary hardware to the households rather than focusing on collective behaviour change, and emphasising the dire need of improved sanitation for healthy living. Such a shift from top-down hardware subsidy driven approach to bottom-up local empowerment was not an easy transition.

There are unique examples in some countries where government officials under compulsion had to promote and popularise a no-subsidy CLTS approach in some areas who provided free hardware sanitation materials and prescribed toilet models in a top-down fashion in other areas in the same district or region, e.g., Madagascar. Such a dichotomy in an approach was due to the conflict between free supplies and subsidised or free distribution, which was totally contradictory and antagonistic to the CLTS approach.

In some parts of West Java province in Indonesia, northeast Madagascar, and a few other countries in Asia and Africa, community-led, people-centred approach to sanitation raised a bigger question on the efficiency and efficacy of investment in rural sanitation, especially focusing on the outcome of public health. The hardware-centred approach to toilet construction in individual households often resulted in the creation of infrastructure, which was highly disappointing and unsatisfactory. People in many places used it for the purpose of storage, a children's study room, or a prayer room etc. Often, open defecation continued in villages nearly covered with 100 percent sanitary toilets in each household built by outside agencies. Questions were raised as to how to improve the hygiene behaviour of the community and to ensure usage of newly created sanitation facilities. Although very slowly, a gradual increase in investment in behaviour change started in the sanitation sector. When some communities received free dole (subsidy money and sanitary hardware) from the government and other outside agencies, and their friends and relatives from the neighbouring villages came to know about it. The message spread very fast. As a result, when a successful triggering of CLTS was done in a village, the neighbouring communities refused to initiate local action to construct toilets by themselves and stop the practice of open defecation. They preferred to wait for the government subsidy for toilet construction while continuing the practice of OD. Village leaders with some vested interest, often called 'Gatekeepers' in some village communities, tried to take advantage of the situation and purposely influenced the triggered community not to construct toilets on their own but to wait for a free supply of materials from the government. They systematically defused the spirit and enthusiasm of the local communities to mobilise themselves and invest to improve their environmental sanitation on their own and get rid of the high incidence of diarrhoea and other enteric diseases. Needless to mention here that the percentage of use of toilets was far too low in villages saturated with free toilets as compared to CLTS-triggered villages. Similar situations were observed in some villages of Ahmednagar and Nanded districts in the state of Maharashtra in India, where the Gram Panchayat (GP) Pradhan (chief of local self-government) responsible for distributing large chunks of government money as sanitation subsidies discouraged the triggered community from digging pits and constructing toilets on their own. They were not prevented from continuing their old practice of OD and wait for the free toilet (often in cash) from the government. Communities followed the village leaders' instructions for fear of losing the opportunity to receive free money and material from the government. This is in contrary to the collective local action initiated by the triggered community, who did not want to wait for a single day but to stop the practice of OD as soon as possible. These Gram Panchayat leaders were afraid of losing government grants and subsidies in the villages within their jurisdiction. The fear was that the triggered community might construct their own toilets, stop OD, and thereby spoil the possibility of receiving free money as government grants to all gram panchayats. Some were also concerned about losing hush money exchanged under the table between the construction contractors and local leaders against work orders for large-scale toilet construction offered through tenders.

During one of the evaluation studies carried out by the World Bank, it was found hundreds of toilet superstructures were constructed in some villages in the state of Gujarat in India under the Total Sanitation Campaign (TSC) and Nirmal Bharat Abhiyan (NBA), which had no substructures at all. When the team randomly inspected some toilets, they did not find any substructure (squatting plate, pan, septic tank, etc.) inside those toilets. Only a cheap superstructure was built. These were done purposefully to fulfil the requirement of the number of toilets planned and constructed with the funds received from the World Bank-supported project with the government. The unscrupulous trick to camouflage and misguide the evaluation mission who often did not inspect the substructure details of all newly constructed latrines meticulously. Rather the team used to carry out a random checking due to paucity of time. The practice of open defecation continued unabated in these area.

As the CLTS approach started spreading rapidly, thousands of ODF communities emerged in more than 72 countries across Asia, Africa, and Latin America. However, districts, regions, and states were far from achieving ODF status in the early years.

After the first decade of CLTS rollout, a large number of communities across the continents declared themselves ODF and demonstrated the power of local community action in drastically reducing the incidence and occurrence of diarrheal diseases. While most of the countries had a large number of ODF villages within the first few years of introduction, ODF districts, regions, and states were very few in number. Some of the important reasons those prevented countries from developing a critical mass of ODF blocks, districts, and regions are as follows:

- Often, ODF villages those emerged from the work of NGOs and CBOs were very few and were spread thinly across the districts or regions. While the NGOs and international development agencies covered their adopted villages and districts with a higher concentration of field staff and uninterrupted flow of funds, clusters of ODF villages emerged like oasis in the desert. Although they served as a glittering example of behaviour change through collective local action, due to a lack of follow up by trained personnel and field facilitators or trained natural leaders, larger areas of the district and region remained unchanged, and a major chunk of the population continued to practice OD. The NGOs and CBOs were of the opinion that covering the entire district was not their responsibility but the commitment of the concerned government department, which often lacked resources to support a large-scale rollout of CLTS covering the entire district or region. Funding support and a lack of trained facilitators were the most important reasons for incomplete and low quality area coverage. With such limitations of spreading out and handling larger areas, often the NGOs, felt that it was the responsibility of the government to ensure total coverage of the districts and regions where they (NGOs) could join hands and extend support.
- Field-level government functionaries and extension workers were not adequately trained and exposed to the CLTS-triggering methodology and post triggering follow-up process. Rather, they were more used to implementing top-down, supply-driven, subsidised, or free toilet construction at the beneficiaries households.
- The CLTS approach was mostly perceived as a theoretical concept, which often became a fad amongst sanitation workers. But many did not have appropriate 'hands-on' training to learn

the skills of facilitation and post-triggering follow-up, leading to the emergence of ODF communities.

- However, the scope and opportunity for CLTS training was limited. Owing to the high demand for CLTS training, only a few senior officers of the government could participate in a few training workshops those were mostly organised by the NGOs. Most of those training courses were designed mainly for the field-level staff and facilitators who were actually responsible for working with the community directly. As CLTS became very popular senior officers from the concerned departments and ministries wanted to avail themselves of the opportunity of receiving hands-on training designed mainly for the field staff. As a result, it was difficult to select right participants from the organizations who would actually use them. As the CLTS Foundation and other training agencies were concerned about the usage and application of knowledge and skills of CLTS after each hands-on training and informed the parent organisations about the crucial importance of appropriate selection criteria of participants for hands-on CLTS training. However, the final decision of selection of institutional participants rested on them. As a result, mostly the senior officers—often missed out the opportunity of receiving hands-on training. Since the CLTS approach, was modern, trendy, and prestigious to know, everybody wanted to be an expert or specialist in it' s methodology.
- Due to a lack of adequate knowledge and understanding of the approach a few senior policy and decision-makers at the higher level of the government (who received at least half or one day orientation training) were not convinced and resisted scaling up CLTS by replacing the traditional top-down approach to sanitation. On the contrary, the regional, district, sub-district and block level officers and field extension staff, understood the efficacy and advantages and outcome of rolling out CLTS

in improving personal hygiene and environmental sanitation and hygiene for improving public health. However, due to the absence of proper official government orders and circulars from the higher authorities, they were constrained to adapt the CLTS approach fully by replacing the ongoing hardware sanitation subsidies for the construction of toilets in each household. In spite of their conviction, they could not shift from subsidised toilet construction to no-subsidy local empowerment for ending the practice of open defecation.

- Adequate exposure on CLTS approach was not arranged for the senior decision-makers and heads of departments of the government as an essential element for scaling up. Neither they were exposed to live demonstrations of CLTS triggering in the field. Most of the efforts were made to develop trainers and facilitators at the community level. This created a void in the understanding of senior-level decision-makers on the efficiency and appropriateness of CLTS approach for faster sanitation coverage. It is for this reason the need for institutional triggering was felt most.

Until the decision-makers were convinced and made appropriate policy changes, the number of ODF villages were few and restricted to some locations within a couple of districts and did not spread across the country.

WHAT IS INSTITUTIONAL TRIGGERING?

Institutional Triggering is an interactive event that involves mobilising institutional support for the CLTS approach with stakeholders within or outside of government agencies and departments that connect directly or indirectly the national/state sanitation policies with the emerging community-led movement directly or indirectly. These actors may come from a range of sectors (ministries/departments), like water and sanitation, health—including public health, local self-government, Gram Panchayats (village councils in India), village communes, national and international NGOs, donor agencies, local institutions, and political leaders. Institutional triggering can also be organised at the regional and district levels, where religious leaders, schoolteachers, community health workers, traditional leaders, and others could participate.

Institutional triggering is aimed at instilling enthusiasm and inspiring the stakeholders to commit and mobilise political will to scale up CLTS across the state or nation and make it ODF. This is achieved by showcasing the success of CLTS villages across the country's subnational and national-level. Institutional actors and policymakers are exposed to the home grown examples of ODF villages and are encouraged to interact face-to-face with the successful communities.

Creating right enabling environment is of crucial importance in the scaling up of CLTS. In order to create confidence and a firm belief in the ability of local people to sustainably change their hygiene behaviour, it is necessary to build the required enabling environment. This is where institutional triggering plays a vital role in initiating necessary corrective measures in sanitation policy and practice for a long-term and tangible health outcome.

The institutional triggering methodology has its own underpinnings in the philosophy and principles of CLTS, which have evolved from years of experience with the uptake of CLTS in various countries. It aims to address the factors that influence the institutional environment and render the smooth implementation of CLTS, particularly in fast-tracking the scaling-up process. Effective and outcome focused facilitation is essential at the early stage of scaling up for effectively generating ODF communities resulting in tangible health outcome. However, the scaling-up of CLTS is often hindered by various factors, like: lack of coordination from institutions at different levels, disbursement of subsidies and free sanitation hardware, lack of dedicated budgets for CLTS, weak policy support, slow/non-responsive public administration, unwilling staff, and a lack of interinstitutional coordination[2].

2 Kamal Kar, *Scaling-Up CLTS*, 2018.

In many countries, there may be several villages that are nearly but not 100% open defecation-free. A special drive and a push by district officials to make an entire district ODF could have a knock-on effect on neighbouring districts, motivating them towards achieving fully ODF district status. This could generate a spirit of healthy competition amongst the districts in a region or state. A strategic approach to achieving at least one ODF district within a region or province as a showcase for encouraging others is crucial but are mostly lacking. The goal of institutional triggering should be to ensure quality in taking CLTS to scale, i.e., to spread from a few isolated examples of ODF villages to widespread adoption. It is essential to have a well-planned, adequately resourced, and coordinated implementation plan backed up by a strong, people-centred national sanitation policy.

As CLTS triggers a community about the consequences of open defecation through evoking emotions of shame and disgust, institutional triggering aims to generate a strong sense of responsibility and obligation amongst the different institutional stakeholders. Inaction and lack of initiative may cause a host of complications within local government and communities particularly where subsidies in sanitation and other development interventions are very pronounced. Poor quality institutionalisation often results in to adoption of nomenclature but transmission of infectious diseases through faecal-oral contamination continues causing huge burden of medical expenses, debility or death, and prolonged financial hardship resulting into social tension. These sufferings and complications are more pronounced amongst the women and children. Preventable diseases such as diarrhoea, cholera, chronic malnutrition, and stunting continue to affect poor communities despite governmental measures to upgrade sanitation infrastructure and primary health coverage.

Institutional triggering serves as a wake-up call for senior policymakers and government officials in national or state institutions working in sanitation and public health. Stakeholders should recognise that apathy towards adopting an appropriate framework for scaling up the CLTS approach and ignoring emerging successful sanitation behaviour change by communities may not necessarily result in reductions in the number of patients suffering from enteric diseases such as diarrhoea, cholera, typhoid, or other prevalent health complications such as malnutrition, undernutrition, and stunting. Public health parameters therefore remain unchanged in spite of adoption of the approach in the national sanitation policy. There are examples of countries or states where, despite household toilet coverage exceeded 70-80 percent yet the percentage of children suffering from malnutrition or stunting remains unchanged due to inconsistent toilet usage, unsafe sanitation practices, and continued practice of OD by some[3].

The process of institutional triggering enables national-level planners and policymakers at the regional and district levels of administration to recognise that CLTS can help achieve faster and more sustainable outcomes by building on successful ODF communities and community-led scaling-up mechanisms, as opposed to building toilets in every household[4]. The institutional triggering process fosters the idea that this does not require investing a lot of money but rather demands a higher level of commitment to strengthening the sanitation policy in support of CLTS and gearing up the field extension machinery appropriately. It requires fulfilling the conditions needed for mainstreaming and scaling up the CLTS process through government officials in districts, sub-districts, and below.

---

3 UNICEF/WHO/World Bank Joint Child Malnutrition Estimates: Stunting (National and Disaggregated). UNICEF and Water Supply and Sanitation in Niger. Water and Sanitation Program, www.wsp.org/sites/wsp/files/publications/CSO-Niger.pdf.

4 Kar K. (2018) *Scaling-Up Community Led Total Sanitation: From Village to Nation*, Rugby, UK: Practical Action Publishing <http://dx.doi.org/10.3362/9781780449753

THE NEED FOR INSTITUTIONAL TRIGGERING

The innovation of CLTS emerged from a process of learning from the local communities as to why they practice OD. This led to the understanding of the factors responsible for large-scale practice of OD from the perceptions of the local communities. This helped in further understanding the reasons behind such practise even when free or subsidised toilets were given to each households. CLTS has spread to more than 72 countries over the last 18 years. Hundreds and thousands of villages and communities became ODF irrespective of their geographical, social, cultural, ethnic, political, or economic diversity[5]. Those communities transformed their collective hygiene behaviour, stopped the practice of OD, and achieved sustainable health gains[6].

However, it should be noted that the success and spread of CLTS have been inconsistent. While thousands of villages across many developing countries declared themselves ODF in the last 15 years, there were very few ODF districts initially. Hardly any ODF regions, provinces, or states existed, except in rural Bangladesh. This necessitated further investigation and analysis to understand why the spread and uptake of CLTS at the district and regional levels were low as compared to the spread at the community level. The discrepancy in the number of fully ODF villages and partially ODF districts and regions was very pronounced. In some countries, more than 80% of the villages in a district achieved ODF status, while the district could not declare itself ODF because there were still a few villages where the practice of OD continued. It was, however, not impossible to change those remaining villages into ODF quickly. However, the challenge was who would trigger those remaining villages and how? Ensuring follow up support

---

5 Kar K. (2018) *Scaling-Up Community Led Total Sanitation: From Village to Nation*, Rugby, UK: Practical Action Publishing <http://dx.doi.org/10.3362/9781780449753

6 Amy Pickering, Amy, et al, "Effect of a Community-Led Sanitation Intervention on Child Diarrhoea and Child Growth in Rural Mali: A Cluster-Randomised Controlled Trial." *The Lancet Global Health*, vol. 3, Nov. 2015, 701–711., www.thelancet.com/action/showPdf?pii=S2214-109X(15)00144-8.

and turning them into ODF to eventually declare the entire district free from open defecation eventually was the main challenge. In most cases, those villages did not belong to the jurisdiction of NGOs working in the districts. So, the question remained as to who would trigger them to move towards ODF status.

It was soon realised that the government need to intervene and take the responsibility. Without government intervention it was likely that the entire district would be deprived from achieving true ODF status and declare itself ODF. The local government's role was to engage itself proactively and do everything needed to transform the remaining villages of the district into ODF. The government could mobilise natural leaders, community consultants, and NGO field staff to trigger the left out villages and achieve full ODF status.

Institutional triggering of the district and regional administration was found to be very effective in filling up these voids. The administration of the district and the region soon realised that more than eighty percent of the work had been done by the local communities themselves and little support and impetus from the government could help the entire district become ODF bringing a lot of glory and fame for them. However in general, apathy and lack of initiative from the district and regional administrations missed out/overlooked the hidden potential capacity of the local communities in supporting the achievement of ODF districts or regional status. In spite of great success attained by their own local communities it was unfortunate, that many districts missed the bus and failed to carry on the enthusiasm, zeal and power of the local communities and take it to scale. Institutional triggering methodology categorically explains such situations, the opportunity cost due to a lack of awareness and initiative often on the part of the district administration.

The challenges and hurdles in replicating the success of local communities' to larger areas? Whose responsibility was it to scale up communities' homegrown success to larger administrative areas?

A number of factors hampered the smooth replication of the success of CLTS from a few villages to wider areas. In the absence of right enabling environment and the proper mechanism for institutionalisation at the national level, scaling up CLTS remained an uphill task. Moreover, weak and unclear sanitation policy failed to stop hardware sanitation subsidies to individual households. This was mainly due to the one-way supply of grant or loan for sanitation infrastructure, with or without interest, provided by the bilateral and multilateral development agencies. Although some governments realised the need for a no-subsidy local empowerment approach for sustained behaviour change and ending the practice of open defecation for good, they could not refuse the free grant or easy loan provided by the donor agencies, which made it difficult for the approach to get institutionalised.

However, due to the absence of any clear mechanism to monitor and regulate the implementation of policy at the ground level, supply of subsidised or free sanitation hardware to households continued sporadically through some INGOs and NGOs. Institutional resistance to no up-front hardware sanitation subsidy to households also played a role in slowing down the scaling-up process. It was difficult to change the mindsets of thousands of sanitation field extension staff, government officials, and civil servants across government agencies, international organisations, and NGOs in favour of a zero-subsidy, bottom-up local empowerment approach to sanitation. This was one of the major reasons that hindered the spread of the CLTS approach[7].

National policymakers and programme managers recognised the fact that safe sanitation played a vital role in the growth and prosperity of a nation, particularly by reducing expenditures on public health,

7 Kar K. (2018) *Scaling-Up Community Led Total Sanitation: From Village to Nation*, Rugby, UK: Practical Action Publishing <http://dx.doi.org/10.3362/9781780449753.

improving income and wealth inequality, facilitating greater social cohesion, and increasing national gross domestic product (GDP)[8].

Communities taking charge of their own lives and changing their hygiene behaviour for collective benefit without waiting for outside help had a strong demonstrable impact on the district, regional, and national-level policy and decision-makers. They realised that the CLTS approach was far more cost-effective and sustainable as compared to traditional approaches to sanitation with the construction of free or subsidised toilets in each household by outside agencies. In the past initiatives to persuade local community to use toilets constructed for free by outside agencies and by stopping the practice of open defecation largely failed to produce expected. On the contrary, when CLTS was triggered, the community understood the crude fact of ingesting one another's faeces as a result of open defection and committed to stop the practice of OD at once. The most important learning from the triggering exercise was the community's realisation through their own visual analysis of the real situation. It emerged as a powerful tool to ignite the community's awareness and collective decision to initiate local action to abandon the practice of OD for the benefit of all. As this involved almost everyone in the community, social solidarity support from the members of the community came along abundantly to translate the communities collective decisions into reality. Along with the expected outcome, many unintended outcomes of the triggering exercise towards sustainable sanitation improvement fascinated all the outsiders including the facilitators every time. There are hundreds of examples of local communities' collective action beyond sanitation to improve their environment, health, livelihood, and social cohesion.

8 Lawrence, J. Joseph, et al. "Beliefs, Behaviours, and Perceptions of Community-Led Total Sanitation and Their Relation to Improved Sanitation in Rural Zambia." *The American Journal of Tropical Medicine and Hygiene*, vol. 94, no. 3, 2016, 553–562., doi:10.4269/ajtmh.15-0335.

During CLTS-triggering exercises, the community through visual analysis using different tools like mapping, calculation of the production and spread of total excreta by the villagers in the open, transect walks, seasonal analysis, faecal-oral contamination route etc. reflects on their present hygiene behaviour practise and its consequences. Realising the terrible impact of OD on everyone especially the children and women they spontaneously decides their own plan of action to end the practice of OD urgently.

At the state or national level, a range of institutional actors plan to improve sanitation policy, design appropriate scaling up strategies, and implementation processes. Due to the absence of any national sanitation policy streamlining and governing sanitation interventions in the country, often actors from various international or national institutions implement sanitation programme focusing their own objectives and approach irrespective of the priorities of the national government. This free for all approach lack the common focus of achieving national ODF status by complementing and supplementing each other in totally eradicating OD through sustained behaviour change. Such haphazard intervention made the scaling-up of the CLTS approach very challenging[9].

With a view to addressing this growing challenge, the institutional triggering methodology was developed by me (Kamal Kar) and used by the CLTS Foundation (initially as trial) since 2013 in a few countries in Asia and Africa. Efforts were made in this approach to influence the policy makers and bring about institutional changes to improve institutional coordination, joint implementation, and scaling-up of the CLTS approach at different levels. It was found to be successful at the national, regional, and district levels in Ghana, Madagascar, East Timor, Benin, Sudan, and the states of Himachal Pradesh and Haryana in India. The methodology was tried out in a few other countries with minor variations and location-specific adjustments. It was from those

9 Kar K. (2018) *Scaling-Up Community Led Total Sanitation: From Village to Nation*, Rugby, UK: Practical Action Publishing <http://dx.doi.org/10.3362/9781780449753.

experiences that the institutional triggering methodology has finally been developed.

TYPOLOGY OF INSTITUTIONAL TRIGGERING

A wide range of institutions are engaged in WASH activities, which differ greatly in their target audience, intervention types, intensity, and focus. While some institutions focus their efforts to improve the sanitation profile of villages, communes, blocks, subdistricts, and districts, others spread their activities in larger geographical areas, covering region, state, or the country. Hence, the design, methodology, and implementation of institutional triggering differ from each other and are planned differently.

In this context, it is important to keep in mind that the preparation, design, plan, preparation and implementation of institutional triggering for the highest levels of leadership involving political leaders, heads of states, senior ministers, departmental officials, or even the President or the Prime Minister are different. The way it is done at the subnational, regional, or district level is different from each other in terms of design, duration, content, facilitation and/or flexibility.

Before planning an institutional triggering, it is important to carefully assess and identify the real challenges and shortcomings of the institutions that hinder the smooth scaling-up of CLTS. In other words, it is important to identify the minor changes and adjustments needed in institutional policy and protocol that might expedite the process of fast-tracking access to sanitation using the CLTS approach. It is important to keep in mind that the focus of the institutional triggering addresses the administrative or logistical bottlenecks in order to change the modalities of their functioning to maximise the homegrown success of communities in minimising open defecation and improving public health and environmental sanitation standards.

Institutional triggering can broadly be classified into three different types based on institutional actors.

- Triggering national institutions
- Regional-level institutional triggering
- Triggering district/subdistrict

Therefore, the outcomes of the three levels of institutional triggering are also different. For example, the outcome of national-level institutional triggering often entails discussion and action planning for policy adjustments, establishment of national standards or norms, budget allocation, modalities of decentralisation, and setting national targets.

Similarly, outcomes for subnational institutional triggering could may include instituting subnational plans, creating a dedicated task force and other administrative adjustments, allocating specific funds, organising hands-on training and capacity-building measures based on progress, issuing directives and guidelines (state-specific guidelines), and fine-tuning the monitoring mechanism. The outcomes of district and local levels of institutional triggering could be different from the above. It is important to bear in mind that the toughest critics of CLTS approach mostly come from this level who oppose the idea of institutionalising CLTS and its countrywide scaling up. They have all reasons for continuing with the subsidised and prescribed external agency led sanitation approach. Institutional triggering is also focused on convincing sceptics about the community empowerment process sustained improvement in personal and environmental sanitation. This is possible to achieve through collective behaviour change of the community and for which capacity-building, improving skills of facilitation, streamlining the implementation, and rolling out of CLTS by harmonising the initiatives of all the major actors of sanitation in accordance with the national and subnational directives are essential. Institutional triggering at this level may be quite similar to community triggering.

INSTITUTIONAL TRIGGERING AT DIFFERENT LEVELS OF GOVERNMENT INSTITUTIONS COMPARED

Criteria	National Level	Subnational/ Regional Level	District Level
1. Institutions whose participation is essential	Government ministries and departments directly or indirectly associated with water and sanitation, donor and lending agencies, bilateral and multilateral organizations, major WASH implementing agencies at the national and subnational level and heads of major NGOs.	Government representatives at the regional/state/subnational level, heads of departments/ ministries at the regional level—WASH, health, education, etc., and heads of major NGOs.	Representatives of the regional government at the district level, heads of departments at the district level—WASH, health, education, etc., and heads of major NGOs working in the district.
2. Participants for the institutional triggering exercise	Prime minister, deputy PM, President, vice President, heads of departments, director generals, and other senior decision-makers from the national level. Participation of ministers and senior officials from more than one ministry responsible for WASH and related areas, e.g., health, education, finance, tourism, environment, state administration, etc., champions from the regional/state level.	Administrative heads of the region/state, heads of departments at the regional/state level, decision-makers at the regional/state level, champions from the district level.	Administrative head of the district and champions from the village/subdistrict level.

3. Extent of coverage	Entire country.	Entire region covering all districts within the region.	Entire district with all the subdistricts, blocks, communes, and villages.
4. Prerequisites for institutional triggering	Many ODF districts in a region and at least 50% of all villages of the remaining district are ODF. The willingness of the highest leadership of region that has demonstrated innovative implementation and funding mechanisms to fast-track sanitation coverage using a community-led approach. Regional level champions like the governor or the deputy governor, heads of departments of a few districts.	Presence of fully or nearly ODF district(s) of the region already evaluated, certified, and declared ODF. At least one/two champions from amongst the senior district level officers willing to share their experience with others.	Presence of clusters of ODF village, blocks, communes, or subdistricts those have maintained the status for at least one year or more.
5. Facilitators/ moderators for the triggering exercise	He/ She should be a well-known trainer /expert in the WASH sector at the national, regional, or international level. With demonstrated result of facilitating ODF districts/regions. Academics without demonstrable results of producing ODF communities field work may not be suitable for this work.	Must be a well-known national level expert/specialist. With significant contribution in the WASH sector. An academician without demonstrable results in countries may not be suitable for this kind of work.	Must be a well-known regional expert or specialist or contributor in the WASH sector. An academician without much demonstrable results in countries may not be suitable for this work.

6. Objectives of institutional triggering	The main objectives of triggering the national level decision-makers are focused: (a) To demonstrate the power of local communities to change their behaviour to eliminate the practice of open defecation and initiate collective local action to improve sanitation. (b) To convince the national leadership to ensure the right enabling environment to multiply the homegrown successful examples of the local communities across the country. (c) To infuse a sense of responsibility in the highest leadership on the need of their role in liberating the nation from the malady of poor sanitation through collective community empowerment at scale.	The objectives to trigger the subnational level decision-makers are focused: (a) To demonstrate the power of local communities to change their behaviour to eliminate the practice of open defecation and initiate collective local action to improve sanitation. (b) To convince the regional leadership to ensure the right enabling environment to multiply the successful homegrown examples of the local communities across the country. (c) To infuse a sense of responsibility in the regional/state leadership on the urgency of realizing their role in accelerating the achievement of ODF status as of one of the first regions/states of the country.	The objectives to trigger the district level decision-makers are focused: (a) To demonstrate the power of local communities to change their behaviour to stop the practice of open defecation and initiate collective local action to improve sanitation. (b) To convince the district leadership to ensure the right enabling environment to multiply the successful examples of the local communities across the country. (c) To infuse a sense of deep interest amongst the district leadership to achieve one of the first ODF districts by themselves.

7. Methodology to be adopted broadly	The methodology used is to compare the sanitation profile of different states and regions of a country, using interactive and participatory analysis depicted visually on the ground. This visual analysis helps the heads of the states or regions discover the cleanest and filthiest states and regions of the country from their own analysis which evoke sense of shame, self-respect, and eventually, a desire to change and improve urgently.	The methodology aims to improve the level of knowledge and understanding of CLTS among stakeholders, and at the same time enhance and provoke their sense of responsibility for solving issues of poor sanitation.	Following the steps mentioned in the column of subnational level, the district level officials will also brainstorm and workout a detailed step-by-step district plan. It is important to note that the synergy of action plan of two adjoining districts should not be overlooked while making the district plans.
8. Content of the triggering exercise to be based on:	The data and information on the present sanitation scenario of the country at the national level. Similar information on WASH from the neighbouring countries in the region to compare with the country concerned.	The data and information on the present sanitation scenario of the region. Similar information from the neighbouring regions to compare with the region concerned.	The data and information on the present sanitation scenario of the district. Similar information from the neighbouring districts to compare with the country concerned.
9. Examples to be used	Case studies, real-life stories, videos from the field triggering exercises and the reaction from the community from different parts of the country.	Case studies, real-life stories, videos from the field triggering exercises and the reaction from the community from different parts of the region.	Case studies, real-life stories, videos from the field triggering exercises and the reaction from the community from different parts of the district.

10. Resource persons/champions to be invited for the exercise	One or two district/regional champions who have made incredible efforts in institutionalizing and scaling-up CLTS across their respective areas.	One or two natural leaders who were identified during these triggering exercises and subsequent presentations at the training giving a strong summary of the triggering and the action plan developed by the village.	District/regional level officers.
11. Focus of the triggering exercise	To instil a sense of ownership amongst the highest political leadership and bring all actors to assume responsibility for improving sanitation and establish convergence of financial and human resources at the national level.	To bring all actors to assume responsibility for sanitation and establish convergence of financial and human resources at the regional level.	Since districts are at the bottom administrative structure, the district magistrate, deputy commissioner, and district development officer are key focal persons responsible to manage the first point of convergence. It is important that the district plans must be prepared with utmost care and sincerity. The success of the implementation at the sub regional or national level would depend largely on the outcome of district plan implementation.

12. Possible outcome of the triggering exercise	i) National sanitation policy reviewed. ii) Appropriate decisions taken to develop interministerial coordination and functional linkages. Highlight and learn from the homegrown examples of ODF villages, districts, and regions. iii) Planning joint visits to successful ODF areas and face-to-face interaction with the ODF community and other champions. iv) Formation of an interdisciplinary and interministerial platform to tackle the issue of ending OD and developing an action plan. v) Finalizing target for achieving ODF national status and chalking out a roadmap for the same. vi) Decisions to modify and fine-tune policy and issuance of necessary orders to the ministry and department, focusing on fast-tracking access to sanitation through local empowerment.	i) Review of the regional/district sanitation policy. ii) Decision to develop a regional/district plan with target and specific budget allocation commitment. iii) Interaction and orientation towards the homegrown community success models. Introduction of natural leaders and bringing them into limelight. iv) Facilitate the development of targets and roadmaps by all subdistrict administrators, for example, bringing together all the district administrators and heads of partner NGOs under the leadership of the provincial governor/ regional minister/administrator in a two-day workshop.	Since districts are the real centres of policy implementation at the grassroots, it involves a lot of changes around the procedures of implementation, staff mobilization, and working mechanisms. If these changes do not commensurate with the changed policy, there will be no outcome on the ground. Merely changing the name of the approach and following the 'business-as-usual' is the worst possible situation that can happen.

	vii) Planning joint visits of senior ministers and officials to neighbouring or other countries where CLTS approach has been institutionalized and adopted in the policy of the government and remarkable results emerged.	The central objective of this workshop is to involve the overall administration of the region in this important issue of sanitation, which generally remains as a neglected and least prioritized agenda. The workshop focuses on conveying the message that poor sanitation is a serious bottleneck to regional prosperity.	
13. Time frame and duration of the triggering exercise	Can't be more than two to four hours depending on the availability and convenience of the senior ministers and senior national level officers from concerned ministries.	Generally, not more than two to four hours depending on the availability of the administrative heads of the region and district level officials from different departments/ministries. However, in countries where the regional administration plays an important role in terms of governance and financing, the exercise could be more extensive, often involving the heads of districts within the region.	Since districts are the real centres of transforming the policy into practice, institutional triggering at this level must be outcome-focused and facilitated skilfully. In order to achieve that, it is often very useful to bring selected natural leaders (NLs) from successful ODF villages and local government officials as resource persons to the workshop.

14. Triggering venue	An ideal venue is a well-known and easy to access conference hall that is not exclusively used by any particular ministry or department. It should be a more common/public venue. Often, the conference hall of a hotel or national and international institutions within the capital city are ideal.	An ideal venue is a well-known and easy to access conference hall that is not exclusively used by any particular ministry or department. It should be a more neutral venue. Often, the conference hall of a hotel or national and international institutions within the regional headquarters are ideal.	An ideal venue is a well-known and easy to access conference hall that is not exclusively used by any particular ministry or department. It should be a more neutral venue. Often the conference hall of a hotel or national and international institutions within the district headquarters are ideal.
15. Flexibility that could be allowed for the triggering exercise	Since participation of top national leaders, senior ministers, and high-level decision-makers' is essential, it is important to maintain a high degree of flexibility of time, number of participants, venue, and duration of the exercise to accommodate important issues that might need to be addressed by them urgently.	It is generally difficult to change and flexibly alter the programme as it involves participation of officials from different parts of the region, who need to plan and travel to the headquarters for the exercise. Any sudden change in the programme may lead to a sharp drop in attendance of key persons.	It is very important to stick to the planned schedule of the programme as it involves officials who are the key implementers of policies at the ground level. Without their understanding and ownership, it is impossible to change the ongoing practice.

16. Responsibility of post-triggering follow-up and linkages	Designated officials from the concerned ministries led by an interdepartmental/ interministerial coordinator elected or appointed by the highest authority. Each participating department or ministry would develop their monitoring network in the regional, district, and subdistrict levels for continuous feedback on the changes happening at different levels.	Designated officials from the concerned departments led by an interdepartmental coordinator elected or appointed by the highest authority of the region. Each participating department would develop their monitoring network in the district and subdistrict levels.	Designated officials from the concerned departments led by an interdepartmental coordinator elected or appointed by the highest authority of the district. Each participating department would develop their monitoring network in the subdistrict levels.

PHASES OF INSTITUTIONAL TRIGGERING IN CLTS

Institutional triggering should not be seen as a 'one-off' event. It involves a series of activities before and after the triggering. Preparatory actions (institutional pre-triggering) are required before the actual triggering activity (institutional triggering) and follow-up afterwards (institutional post-triggering follow-up). The process of institutional triggering can be divided into two phases.

The first phase of institutional triggering aims to establish a collective understanding among the stakeholders about the complexities involved in scaling-up of the CLTS approach to work towards achieving national/regional ODF status. It also attempts to instill the realisation of collective institutional responsibility of achieving universal access to sanitation. Another objectives of this phase is to trigger the realisation amongst the key stakeholders on the importance and urgency of achieving the status of a clean and ODF nation through nationwide sanitation campaign that would help every ministry to reach their goals. It is thus a step towards making sanitation everyone's responsibility rather than imposing it on the government, or any one agency or institution.

The second phase of institutional triggering aims to draw out a collective institutional action plan to launch ODF at scale. This might result in the initiation of a roadmap for change, which includes a target date for achieving a clear goal covering substantial administrative area, such as a district or a region, involving all communities in that area. During the institutional triggering by the senior decision-makers (eg: Chief Minister/Governor/Commissioner of a state) who call for an urgent meeting of all senior staff members and concerned agencies to discuss and, initiate urgent action and prepare way forward plan. Such reactions and immediate actions by the senior decision makers signals success of institutional triggering exercise. Like CLTS, Institutional Triggering is also an outcome focused exercise. Preparation of a properly laid-out roadmap, a realistic intra- and inter-institutional collaborative action plan, appropriate budget allocation, and fixing a target date of launch and ODF declaration by the districts and the regions are likely to accelerate the progress towards securing sustainable national ODF status. Each actor must recognise their respective institutional role and share with others to hasten up the process of achieving national ODF status.

The details of the methodology will be discussed in Section 2 of this book.

CHALLENGES OF SCALING UP OF CLTS APPROACH THOSE CAN BE ADDRESSED BY INSTITUTIONAL TRIGGERING

There could be barriers for smooth scaling-up of CLTS which could be addressed by institutional triggering. These are mostly challenges related to institutional policy, effective mechanisms of policy implementation, issuance of government orders, and appropriate fund allocation. Often, due to a lack of proper monitoring and implementation at the ground level remains unchanged even when CLTS is adopted as a policy at the national level.

Institutional triggering primarily raises the following questions:

- Why the number of ODF communities are limited to just a few hundred or less within a country, years after it is successfully implemented in some areas of the country?
- Why all the districts, regions, and the entire country did not become ODF and are far from achieving hundred percent ODF status?
- What stops a nation from achieving countrywide ODF status when the local communities have the capacity to change?

The critical question is whether the national-level institutions can trigger local communities across the country to benefit from CLTS. Addressing these issues is the primary focus of institutional triggering which lies at the heart of all these activities. Slow progress towards achieving ODF national status often results from a lack of initiative at the highest level of decision-makers. When asked, whether it would be possible to achieve ODF national status, often the answers of senior officials and decision-makers (eg: countries like East Timor, Ghana, Madagascar, Mozambique and a few others) were affirmative. In all these countries, the senior decision-makers expressed their intent desire to reach the goal as quickly as possible. However, a few reasons that prevented these countries from achieving ODF status, as expressed by senior government officials were as follows:

1. INADEQUATE OR PARTIAL UNDERSTANDING OF CLTS AMONGST SENIOR DECISION-MAKERS

One of the common hurdles to the quality scaling-up of CLTS in some countries was found to be a lack of clear understanding of the approach amongst the senior decision and policy makers. Often, their understanding is influenced by a preconceived notion that the poor could never afford to purchase sanitary hardware nor invest to construct their own toilet. It was only possible to have toilet if it was constructed free of cost at each household by the government or NGOs. Accordingly hundreds of thousands of toilets were built by the international development agencies, bilateral, multilateral, INGOs and others all over Africa, Asia and Latin America. Unfortunately most of those toilets were never used for the purpose they were built and mostly ended up as chicken coop, store room and different other uses. Open defecation continued as usual[10]. Often, such traditional conviction were further by the thought that open defecation does not cost money or require any investment by the poor. Hence, external subsidy or the supply of free toilets was thought as the only way to shift millions to toilets/latrines

---

10 Kar, K and Pasteur, P. (2005) *'Subsidy or self-respect? Community- Led Total Sanitation: an update on recent developments'*, IDS Working Paper 257, Brighton: Institute of Development Studies.) Such mindset of development intervention in sanitation guided the national and international development agencies over decades.

from the practice of OD. Such understanding is often influenced by the following mindset:

- Inadequate understanding and absence of felt need for safe sanitation by the poor different categories of population living in rural, urban and semi-urban areas in developing countries was thought to be the result of illiteracy and a total lack of awareness about the health of their own families including women and children.
- Inability to invest money and resources for construction of toilets according to designs prescribed by the government, NGOs and other outside agencies. Generally, permanent/semi-permanent civil structures were prescribed for construction of externally designed toilets which costed more money. For example VIP (Ventilated Improved Pit) latrines were prescribed in almost all countries of Africa and Asia in the early 50s and 60s by UNICEF, UNDP and other INGOs[11]. Prescribed latrine models were constructed free of cost or cost sharing basis (by labour contribution by the beneficiary). Often these became a burden on the beneficiary. However, the percentage of use of the VIP latrines were found to be very low[12].
- Lack of easy access to sanitary hardware and technical support by the community living in remote rural areas far from the urban market. Often the cost of transporting a set of toilet hardware (RCC rings, squatting plate, toilet pan and gas pipe etc.) was more than the cost of all these sanitary hardware. Moreover there was always the risk of damage or breakage of these materials during transport by bullock cart or other rural means of transport.

---

11 https://documents1.worldbank.org/curated/en/363321468591320803/pdf/266220PAPER0English0Blue0gold0no-04.pdf?_gl=1*1c9t480*_gcl_au*MTQyNzUwNzQxMy4xNzI2ODI0NDA2

12 https://iwaponline.com/wpt/article/14/4/825/69881/Design-and-construction-of-household-ventilated

Based on these assumptions, free or subsidised sanitary hardware was provided by international agencies and many other national development agencies including the governments. While the emphasis was on building sanitation infrastructure, the importance and urgency of individual and collective behaviour change was often missing. As a result, hundreds and thousands of unused toilets constructed by outside agencies free of cost for the population were found to be scattered all over the rural landscapes of the developing world. These expensive infrastructures remained mostly unused and ended up as garbage dump, chicken coops, livestock sheds, storage rooms, and many others.

A remarkable example I heard was from Togo, where the Principal of a rural school shifted his office to the newly built toilet block constructed by UNICEF. Obviously, that was the only and best civil structure available in the school campus. Where all the other buildings of the school had mud walls and thatched roofs, toilet was a nice and permanent civil structure. The school principal was excited and happy to occupy the newly constructed and brightly painted toilet block as his new office. The building which was constructed as a toilet for the children turned into Principal's office. The children of the school continued to pee and defecate in the bushes around the school as before.

The struggle for quality scaling-up in many countries was focused to educate the higher-level officials and explain the principles of CLTS, specifically the power of collective local action by the communities as an effective approach to sustainable sanitation.

Institutional Triggering's potential to reach hundreds of thousands of people in a cost-effective and sustainable way was underestimated. This was especially true for the senior decision-makers, who had the authority to influence the national budget and allocation of fund for different sectors including WASH. Often, sanitation receives a low priority in budget allocation as compared to water. Although the need for creating a separate ministry for Sanitation and Hygiene has been felt and demand raised by the sanitation and hygiene professionals it didn't received adequate attention. Barring a couple of countries, (Ethiopia,

Kenya and a few countries) sanitation and hygiene continued to remain as a department or directorate in the Ministry of Water or Health or Public Health[13]. However, the influence of these people could helped in rapidly spreading the success of CLTS for quick improvement of the sanitation profile across districts, regions, or countries.

Generally, the trained technical staff of WASH understands the essentials of the CLTS approach, its process and application of the tools. However, due to a lack of policy support and administrative and financial backing from the district or regional administrations, the CLTS approach encounters serious hindrances and setbacks in scaling up and often fails to harness its full potential.

> *The realization over the years is that governments are not willing to make seismic changes to the enabling environment for CLTS alone - the common thinking is that CLTS and resulting hardware are the dominion of households and the private sector (this was literally something said by the Nigerian Minister but echoed by the reality of investments and engagements across countries globally in rural sanitation). There is no interest in making substantive public rural sanitation investments/engagements as long as the level of service is household self-supply. Introducing the concept of 'safety' is what we are finding is shifting the narrative – it implies a government role in regulation, services delivery (even if just setting standards and enforcing them) as well as monetary implications. This is what is being done in the Game Plan and it's been effective in deepest CLTS countries in WCAR. While we are not calling it triggering, we are using a series of catalytic interventions to stimulate and engage governments to think about what is needed to safeguard public safety, strengthen data, policies and coordination structures to deliver safe services.*
>
> – *Vision and perspective of a senior UN WASH expert*

13 Initiative of the Ministry of Water 'De loe' in Madagascar needs to be mentioned here and Annexed.

Example: Mozambique

In Mozambique, Ms. Deolinda Vissai Paulo Bengura Cheche, ex-district administrator of the district of Manica Province, accompanied the CLTS Rapid Appraisal Protocol (CRAP) team to the Regional Governor's office for a meeting on May 5, 2015. During the debriefing meeting with the team, the provincial governor was pleasantly surprised to learn from the district administrator about the way she had successfully introduced, implemented, and scaled up CLTS across all villages in her district, which eventually helped the district achieve ODF status. It was an embarrassment for the governor, who did not know about such an innovative and powerful example of achieving an ODF district with the local community's participation in his own province. The governor was especially embarrassed to learn that he knew so little about the districts of the province he was governing. He was also unaware of the CLTS programme initiated by the local NGO, as they did not contact him or inform him but started working directly with the district authorities.

The above example from Manica province of Mozambique clearly indicated that a lack of policy support and administrative and financial back up from the national/regional level often subpress the emergence of many enthusiastic champions of CLTS spontaneously and scale up the homegrown success of CLTS. This was the reason for sporadic emergence of ODF villages within a country rather than large scale area coverage of contiguous villages and districts at a reasonable pace.

Example: Ghana

In Ghana, CLTS implementation at the district level is funded by the District Assembly, and decisions about fund allocations are made by the District Coordinating Executive (DCE) and the District Coordinating Director (DCD). District Environmental Health

> Officers, who used to facilitate CLTS, had to struggle for funds, which were rarely disbursed in time. Although they trained many facilitators and organised training workshops, they had to manage the events with great difficulty because of the non-availability of funds in time. They were unable to travel to communities for fresh triggering and post-triggering follow-up visits as a basic requirement for hands-on CLTS training. It became apparent that funds were being allocated to other activities because the DCEs and DCDs were unaware of the CLTS approach and thus never prioritised it. Furthermore, at the regional level, regional ministers and regional executive officers had a very poor understanding of CLTS and never asked for any updates on the progress of sanitation in their districts. Although the DCEs and DCDs were reporting to the regional executive officers, they often did not share their experience of CLTS with others. Often they thought that sharing the experience of CLTS might be a conflicting idea against prevailing government policy of top-down hardware-centric sanitation subsidy driven approach.
>
> *From the report of CLTS Foundation's field staff who worked in different regions of Ghana during 2013–14.*

The example from Ghana illustrates that how the government officials of the line departments struggled hard to scale up very successful examples of CLTS to different districts and regions. The details of Ghana example has been discussed in page number 73 and 184. Their efforts could have yielded highly encouraging results had government institutions and other political decision-makers been supportive. Field-level CLTS staff could have continued their struggle if there had been clear official guidelines endorsed by the higher-ups. Institutional triggering is principally used to raise awareness amongst senior institutional actors to increase their support and commitment to CLTS within their administrative jurisdictions.

This highlighted the lack of communication between departments and ministries, development agencies, and government administration at different levels. In such situations, the success of CLTS remained an isolated event, and the administrators were ignorant about the potential of scaling up CLTS by the empowered communities themselves.

The CLTS Foundation team had a similar experience during an institutional triggering exercise in Zambezia province in Mozambique. The Provincial Governor did not have a clear understanding of the non-negotiable principles of CLTS and how to propagate the idea of collective local action in the community.

This clearly demonstrated that homegrown examples, which often remained unobserved and missed out by the district or the regional administration. As a result, the success of community empowerment developed in the district did not cross the boundary of the district and reached the neighbouring districts for further replication and scaling up as a desired outcome. Often, the neighbouring districts or regions reinvented the same wheel again.

2. WEAK POLICY CONTEXT

The full potential and impact of CLTS is never harnessed and often gets obscured unless a strong policy and supportive environment is ensured. The government's policy commitment to CLTS contributes to smoother and faster scaling up in a number of ways. First, it can encourage all agencies working on sanitation within the country to use Community Led (CLTS) approach as the nationally adopted and approved methodology to proceed forward in sanitation which is not possible in a weak policy environment. Second, it can ensure that the practice of providing upfront household hardware subsidy is eliminated altogether, as all NGOs and other agencies are aligned within a common framework for practice. The central idea of sequencing the steps is to bring the horse before the cart. Sanitation hardware supply and support is initiated after collective behaviour change in the community. Third, the national sanitation policy needs to be followed by an implementation framework, which should clearly define the details of steps and actions to be initiated at different levels for sustainable scaling up CLTS across the country. The framework should include the roles and responsibilities, implementation guidelines, sources of funding, verification protocols, and alike for both the government and other implementing institutions. Institutional triggering could be used at the highest level to mobilise a policy process that supports CLTS.

Example: Madagascar

The CLTS Foundation facilitated the very first institutional triggering in the Diana region of Madagascar, where the Regional Governor and the senior decision-making officials participated in a two day workshop. It is important to mention here that the traditional top down supply driven and hardware centric sanitation programme at the household level was being implemented in this region. This example of a dichotomy in policy and its consequences were presented and discussed in the triggering meeting at the national level. The idea was to present a comparative analysis of the two approaches including their cost effectiveness, community participation and sustainability to all participants of the workshop at the beginning[14]. The radical changes that took place after the triggering exercise fast-tracked Diana region's progress in sanitation remarkably. Within a few months, the region picked up speed and achieved significant progress to be at par with other regions of the country.

14 Institutional Triggering Workshop report of Diana region, Madagascar.

3. ABSENCE OF INNOVATIVE FUNDING MECHANISMS

Considering the powerful impact that CLTS can have in achieving ODF communities and its positive outcomes[15], the requirement of funds for rolling out CLTS is minimal as compared to the implementation and scaling up of conventional approaches to sanitation. The key inputs required to roll out CLTS are primarily trained and skilled human resources with the right attitude and behaviour to work with the rural and urban communities with a sound knowledge and understanding of all four stages of CLTS, i.e., pre-triggering, triggering, post-triggering follow-up, and post-ODF activities. Additionally, flexible funding is required for the implementation of all activities in the four stages of implementing CLTS. However, often in many large-scale government programmes in developing countries, funds are allocated for triggering activities alone, and the other equally important aspects of post-triggering follow-up and post-ODF sustainability are overlooked or neglected. Incomplete application of all four essential steps of CLTS often fails to maintain the collective spirit and enthusiasm generated by the community during the triggering exercise and to sustain the behaviour change. Therefore, required funds for the mobility of local staff to visit the communities for meetings, triggering, post-triggering follow-up, and post-ODF activities are essential, which would contribute greatly to developing truly empowered communities. Some of the empowered communities would emerge as role models which would spontaneously inspire and encourage adjoining local communities to do the same. At any cost this important aspect of mobility of field staff to the triggered communities needs to be ensured.

Lack of flexible funding for community facilitation is often seen in countries having a weak policy and a poor understanding of CLTS approach among the policymakers. This is common in countries where sanitation hardware continues to be the most important and sole item of

---

15 https://www.cedlas.econo.unlp.edu.ar/wp/wp-content/uploads/mali-clts-impact-evaluation-2014.pdf

expenditure in the national sanitation budget. In projects where a small percentage of the budget is allocated for software support, like behaviour change etc. it is generally administered as a top-down instruction to the field staff which comes as a education package of health and hygiene. Generally, this information package is administered to the communities in a top down teaching mode, which defeats the very purpose and spirit of "community- led" CLTS. Institutional triggering could be a very effective tool in convincing senior policy and decision makers about the need and urgency for creating an innovative funding mechanism for CLTS.

A majority of countries have policies for WASH in health care facilities, but they are not supported with sufficient human or financial resources.

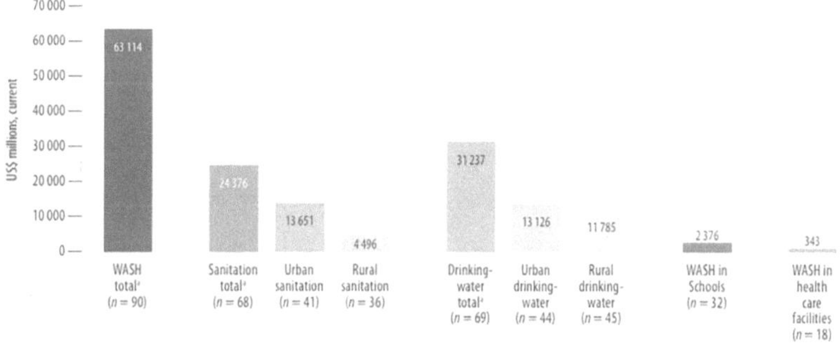

[a] WASH total includes the estimated costs of sanitation and drinking-water plans, as well as plans that could not be disaggregated between sanitation and drinking-water. Sanitation and drinking-water totals include the estimated costs of urban and rural plans, as well as plans that could not be disaggregated between urban and rural areas.

Source: GLAAS 2021/2022 country survey.

Percentage of countries that reported policies for WASH in health care facilities supported by resourced plans (n = 118)

4. INSTITUTIONAL OPEN DEFECATION

'Institutional Open Defecation' is a term coined by me (Kar, 2018) to denote some other approaches to sanitation those are often contradictory to each other and differ on the principles, spirit and methodology of implementation of CLTS. These are also confusing in spreading the message of local empowerment and often flawed with high external input-oriented paternalistic mode of development. Such confusion exists between two diagonally opposite types of participation, viz., *participation for material incentives and self-mobilization*[16]. Even a rumour of distribution of subsidy in cash or kind (sanitation hardware) to any section of the population, spreads fast and tends to diffuse the spirit of collective local action not only in the already triggered community but in the neighbouring communities as well. This seriously damages any attempts to facilitate CLTS or initiate any community led collective initiatives. The reason is that the people's expectation goes up and the wait for the subsidy money or free material rather than initiating immediate action to stop the practice of OD by constructing simple latrines using their own labour and minimal resources. This is a major hindrance to scaling up of CLTS. That is why it is of utmost importance to have a uniform and commonly agreed national sanitation policy governed and guided by a proper implementation framework and easily implementable mechanism.

Institutional open defecation often results from a non-existent or weak national sanitation policy, coupled with total absence of policy implementation mechanisms. If at all there exists any such policy—often due to non-adherence of directives by all agencies, improper interinstitutional coordination and undefined roles and responsibilities of the concerned bodies the so called norms—remains useless and non-functional.

Example: Ghana

The CLTS Foundation team visited a community near Tamale in the northern region of Ghana in 2013. Local environmental health staff were concerned about a situation where the community was triggered several times with no success in motivating people to take action and stop the practice of OD. The field staff requested the CLTS Foundation team to visit the area and suggest way forward. It was

16 Pretty, J. (1995) Participatory learning for sustainable agriculture, World Development, 23 (8), 1247–1263.

observed that concrete latrine slabs were found scattered in places around the village, with signs and logos of different institutions marked on them with dates. However, very few latrines were seen to be constructed using those slabs, and other materials. Instead of using the latrine construction materials, people continued to defecate in the open. The learning from the experience was that by simply dumping' sanitary hardware at the communities doorstep without triggering behaviour change results in waste of precious resources. Dumping material for constructing free toilets at each household of the community members might be useful in some way, but certainly not for the purpose for which they were given to them. Many people used the rings as cattle mangers, and the toilet room as storehouses, kiosk or grocery shops, etc. Such a free supply of materials also raised the community's expectations and killed the spirit of taking spontaneous collective action for any social or behavioural change. Mindset to receive free supply of materials from outsiders deepened. In such situations, often the community preferred to wait for the free dole rather than changing themselves on their own felt need.

Lack of institutional coordination amongst the major actors of sanitation was found to be one of the main reasons for failure to achieve ODF national status in many countries. Often, the responsibility of ensuring collective behaviour change to stop the practice of open defecation was considered to be the sole responsibility of the water and sanitation/health department or ministry. Such a huge task of transforming the age-old behavioural pattern of the entire nation cannot easily be achieved by the effort of one ministry or department alone. This calls for joint and collective ministerial action backed by a strong political will from the highest level of leadership of the country. Lack of understanding of the local environment and undermining the traditional values of the diversified structure of caste and creed of the community could be a bottleneck to sustaining positive outcome of CLTS. For example, households of higher castes (e.g., Brahmins)

Hindu family in India or Nepal used to go far away from homes to defecate. While defecating, they wrap the sacred thread around their ear and take bath in nearby river or pond after reliving themselves. After bath they wear clean clothes before returning home. All these were possible when the population density was not very high and a lot of empty space was available in and around the villages. However, with the increase in population, such open spaces were not available anymore, and the need for safe sanitary latrine became a dire necessity. There are instances in the states of India where well-off and rich people used to go far away by their cars or motorcycles, release themselves, wash, and come back home. Although many of them had nice water-sealed sanitary toilets with attached bathrooms, etc. at home. The basic thought of defecating in the very close proximity to a dwelling house or in a bedroom attached toilet was considered unhygienic and unethical by many traditional families. However, it took time for the mind-set of the traditional rural community to change and reflect from the parlance of collective behaviour change. For a long time, the hygiene behaviour and the practice of OD by the better-off and rich landlords, including higher-caste people, differed greatly from those of the so-called lower-caste, poor, and migratory populations.

Often, the institutions operate in isolation from each other, restrict their activity within the geographical area of their work, and lack synergy and coordination with other partners towards achieving the ultimate objectives of making an ODF nation. In several countries, I witnessed situations where certain institutions (welfare-oriented NGOs, populist political institutions) continued to provide subsidies or free supply of sanitary hardware to households. e.g. Ghana material assistance even when the national policy prohibited them. Many of these subsidised or free sanitary hardware items are often seen lying unused around the community, where the practice of OD continued. Additionally, this created serious hindrance to the successful implementation and rollout of CLTS by other agencies working with the community led collective approach in line with the government's sanitation policy.

Development agencies (mostly NGOs) working on sanitation have different strategies and methods of intervention. Most of the interventions are made by providing direct material support in terms of sanitation hardware, providing cash to households or constructing the full toilet free of cost. Of course the construction of the toilet follows externally prescribed engineering design and construction materials brought from outside. As a result it was not uncommon to find different models of toilets in the villages provided by different organisations. Some toilets were more expensive than others in the same village. As mentioned earlier not all organisations constructed the toilets fully but supplied construction materials only e.g. bricks, cement, toilet pans, connecting and ventilation pipes etc. The responsibility of construction rested on the beneficiary who were supposed to bear the cost of labour and mason. As a whole there used to be many variations in all aspects of free or subsidised toilets given to the community. Due to the absence of any regulatory agency in the game it used to be a free for all situation. Perhaps the only commonality was that most of all these toilets were not used.

As the above mentioned the practice of sticking to their respective policies, plans, and approaches of implementation in isolation from others there was no institutional thought or initiative to follow a commonly agreed homogenous approach has been termed 'Institutional Open Defecation'. Such a practise leads to a chaotic situation where the community at the receiving end gets thoroughly confused and become a passive recipient of help and support from outside agencies. Not only the local communities had a chance to mobilise their collective local strength in the campaign of stopping OD but never felt that it was their own programme for the benefit of all the members of community. It always remained as a outsiders programme. As a result the development intervention becomes more dependent on external input oriented supply driven phenomena. The strength of participation of the local community erodes fast and make the initiative as one-off development intervention with no sustainability.

5. HUMANITARIAN CONFLICT AND EMERGENCY CONTEXT

International humanitarian and welfare organisations including development NGOs, and INGOs often provide material and financial support to internally displaced and migrated communities from conflict zones, areas of natural disasters, or other emergency situations. Communities flee from their settlements in and around conflict zones to new location for safety, leaving behind their properties. In bigger conflict zones, where thousands of families with women and children move to new locations receive help and support from the international development agencies like UNHCR, Islamic Relief Society, Red Cross etc. who work for the rehabilitation and welfare of displaced persons and arrange their basic needs like shelter, food, water, and sanitation.

Example: Bangladesh

In 2016, adequate WASH facilities would have prevented worldwide, 1.9 million deaths as well as uncountable life years of suffering by sick people (expressed in 123 million disability adjusted life years) as consequence of WASH-related diseases (WHO *et al.* 2020[17]). The same source also asserts that shockingly 13% of deaths in children under the age of 5 years were related to the same causes. Despite several improvements that have been done over the years, inadequate access to clean WASH remains a major global concern in refugee camps putting refugees at high risk of communicable diseases. It has been reported that only 30% of WASH services have been reaching the Rohingya population. Only a fraction of the 9 million litres of clean water the refugee and drought affected population worldwide would need every day, is being made available (Islam & Nuzhath 2018[18]). Due to inadequate WASH facilities and growing population density in these sites, the risk of pathogen dissemination and the

17 https://www.who.int/publications/i/item/9789240006416
18 https://jogh.org/documents/issue201802/jogh-08-020309.pdf

spread of various communicable diseases continues to increase also among Rohingya refugees.

Interviews with WASH-related organizations confirmed several WASH attributable infections among the refugee population, such as bloody diarrhoea, cholera, skin infection, unexplained fever, acute respiratory infection (ARI), other respiratory issues, and had identified 224,145 confirmed cases of acute water diarrhoea. In Bangladesh, more than 836 000 Rohingya refugee population is in need of humanitarian assistance[19]. These refugees faced discrimination in their native land in terms of various restrictions imposed on them due to the effective denial of their citizenship. This led to several human rights violations including limited access to health care services[20]. Currently they are under significant health risks and it has become a challenge to address their health needs. Due to the increasing number of Rohingya refugees and their congested living conditions in camps, there has been an overwhelming increase in their health risks[21]. Refugees and affected community require 9 million litres of safe water daily, and water, sanitation and hygiene (WASH) services are reaching only 30% of the Rohingya people in need. Thus leaving them with no other option than to fetch dirty water from muddy streams. 85% of the refugees still have no access to latrines[22]. All of which in turn increases the risk of communicable disease outbreak. There has been reports of measles outbreak amongst new arrivals, the number of cases

19 Intersector Coordination Group. Situation Update: Rohingya Refugee Crisis Cox's Bazar. Intersector Coordination Group; 2018.

20 Watch HR. World Report 2017. Available: http://www.hrw.org/world-report/2017. Accessed: 30 October 2017.

21 United Nations Children's Fund. Outcast and Desperate: Rohingya refugee children face a perilous Future. New York: UNICEF; 2017

22 United Nations High Commissioner for Refugees. Operational Update-Bangladesh. Geneva: UNHCR; 2017.

reported is 419[23]. The largest oral cholera vaccination was held in the refugee camps and even though it was able to reach 100% of the targeted population, the risks of waterborne and other infectious diseases are still exceptionally high due to their unhygienic living conditions[24]. Diphtheria outbreak has resulted in 38 deaths and more than 5800 suspected cases of diphtheria have been reported as of February 2018[25]. There have also been reports on respiratory problems and skin diseases among the refugees who have arrived since 25th August-with 10846 and 3422 cases respectively.

Among the refugees, 720000 are children[26]. 14740 orphan Rohingya children have been identified since September 20, 2017 in the settlements in Ukhia and Teknaf[27]. An estimated 250000 children under the age of 8 require life-saving interventions through community-based activities such as vaccination campaigns whereas 240000 children under-five years need malnutrition prevention and treatment support through nutritious supplementary food.16965 children with severe acute malnutrition (SAM) require inpatient and outpatient treatment. 204000 adolescent girls need nutritional support and 237500 children from 6 months to 15 years need to receive measles-rubella (MR) vaccine.

23 United Nations Children's Fund. Bangladesh Humanitarian Situation report-10 (Rohingya Influx). New York: UNICEF; 2017

24 World Health Organization. Weekly Situation Report. Bangladesh: WHO; 2018.

25 United Nations High Commissioner for Refugee. Disease threatens refugees in Bangladesh in unplanned sites. Geneva: UNHCR; 2017

26 Women UN. Gender Brief on Rohingya Refugee Crisis Response in Bangladesh. New York: UN Women; 2017.

27 United Nations Children's Fund. Bangladesh Humanitarian Situation report-8 (Rohingya Influx). New York: UNICEF; 2017.

After the end of the conflict, when these communities are asked to return to their original location, often they refuse to do so and demand continued external support for food, water, sanitation, and other basic needs. Often, these communities do not want to move out of the comfort zone created by outside development agencies. It then becomes difficult for international organisations to withdraw the material support as the community becomes habituated to receiving free supply of material for a long period of time. This happens in the water and sanitation sectors as well. In the absence of a systematic withdrawal strategy, it often becomes difficult to change the mindset of dependency in people who are used to receiving free supply of food and materials for years. The sanitation situation in hundreds of IDPs (Internally Displaced Persons) or refugee camps in conflict zones is deplorable, as there is no ownership of the sanitary infrastructure provided by the rehabilitation agencies which results in to terribly filthy toilets and surrounding areas. Often, this leads to sudden outbreak of waterborne diseases like diarrhoea, cholera, and typhoid in these communities.

Institutional triggering in such cases would be an appropriate intervention, which would influence and convince institutional actors to come together and work out a strategy of intervention that focuses on building collective hygiene behaviour change through capacity building and other related activities amongst the displaced population. A good strategy is to ensure that the communities gradually get prepared to take the responsibility of WASH management by themselves, moving away from long-term dependency on others.

Example: Sudan

In Sudan, 5.4 million people, out of a population of 35 million (about 13%), are estimated to be in need of humanitarian assistance, predominantly caused by continued armed conflict in Darfur, South Kordofan, and Blue Nile State. The ongoing crisis in South Sudan has resulted in an increased influx of South Sudanese refugees, primarily in White Nile, South Kordofan, West Kordofan, Blue Nile, and Khartoum states. The humanitarian community provides assistance to many of these refugee camps with food assistance, shelter, water, and sanitation. Although emergency WASH assistance usually includes building latrines, in the IDP camps across the Darfur region of Sudan, the sanitation situation is grim. There are not enough latrines for the huge population. Easy access to soap and water for the tens of thousands of displaced people currently living in the camps is scanty. The latrines that exist are quickly filling up, with no systematic plan in place to empty and dispose of the excreta once the latrines fill up. Many of these latrines are unhygienic, with excreta visible around and outside the latrines, which exposes the people, especially the children, to contamination. It is also a reality that the number of latrines available is simply not enough to accommodate the number of people living in these camps, as a result many people are defecating in the open. These precarious conditions put the children in these conflict areas at high risk of catching dysentery, cholera, and hepatitis.

The humanitarian and development communities are struggling to find an appropriate strategy to trigger behaviour change amongst these communities and ensure that each household eventually builds their own toilet. In some of the longer-term IDP communities, CLTS has been applied with some success. In newer settlements, there is potential to instill self-reliance among the population through collective behaviour change approach. This, however, needs an integrated and coordinated implementation strategy by the government and international agencies engaged in ensuring safe sanitation and public health of these areas.

6. WASH AND CLIMATE CHANGE

Rapid climate change resulting into increased frequency and intensity of extreme weather conditions have been impacting directly on the delivery of WASH services globally. For instance, drought reduce water availability disrupting all water reliant WASH systems rising of sea levels and frequent flooding increase the risk of contamination from overflowing of sanitation systems and extreme heat events change water consumption and efficiency of sewerage treatment processes. Climate hazards not only affect the wash services but often result in people using unsafe sources of water and reverting to the practice of open defecation as they are unable to maintain good hygiene practises causing WASH related disease outbreaks. The growing risk of climate change badly affecting the wash services are not necessarily addressed by a majority of countries. Ofcourse there are other climate change related challenges that pose threat to scaling up CLTS through sustained behaviour change towards safe sanitation.

According to the Glass report 2021/2022 a country survey reveals that:

- Only 20% of countries implement climate change preparedness approach in WASH at the local level
- 25% implement at just a few pilots or model sites
- 55% do not implement at all

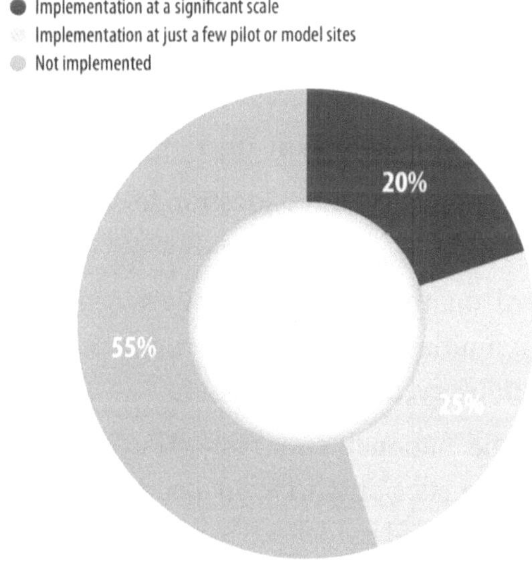

Source: GLAAS 2021/2022 country survey.

Level of implementation of climate change preparedness approaches for local-level risk assessment and management of WASH (n = 118)

Around the world, there are people who are disproportionately affected by climate change[28]. Billions of people lack safely managed WASH services and are therefore already extremely vulnerable, leaving them at higher risk from climate shocks and unable to respond effectively to such shocks. Others live in areas that are vulnerable to droughts, wildfires, coastal storms or sea level rise. Governments should take actions to identify populations disproportionally affected by climate change and ensure sustained access to WASH services.

7. WEAK OR UNCLEAR STRATEGY FOR TAKING CLTS TO SCALE

Often, in countries with a clearly defined national sanitation policy that supports CLTS, successful implementation is hindered due to a lack of effective policy implementation mechanisms. While a few successful examples of CLTS can be found in a country, plans to achieve large-scale ODF district or regional coverage are often absent.

A weak national sanitation strategy is generally characterised by the following:

1. Absence of a clearly laid rollout plan and directives for CLTS implementation in the region, district, or subdistrict.
2. There is no specific budget allocation for scaling up CLTS.
3. Monitoring indicators for measuring the progress of sanitation are focused on the number of toilets constructed rather than ODF communities. As a result, the change in collective behaviour remains unobserved and missed out.
4. Although the national sanitation strategies of some countries emphasise 'no-subsidy CLTS', in reality, toilets are constructed following prescribed models with free supply of sanitary hardware

28 "Populations disproportionally affected by climate change" was not defined in the GLAAS 2021/2022 country survey, as different countries have different definitions of these populations.

materials by the government. It is also interesting to note how, in a few countries, no paradoxically-subsidy CLTS and top-down subsidised toilet construction are implemented side by side.

5. Undermining the power of collective local action of the community and existing social solidarity by upfront external material or financial help often aborts the element of local empowerment. In such cases, although the community moves towards achieving ODF status, being allured by free or subsidised material incentives, they often slip back to the practice of OD. This might destroy the traditional social solidarity mechanisms of the community instigating or provoking a mindset of 'uppers' and 'lowers' between the rich and the poor or between the 'upper' and 'lower' caste. Such mental differences often jeopardises the old, traditional communal values of self-help.

Estimated annual costs of plans and strategies for drinking-water are higher than those for sanitation.

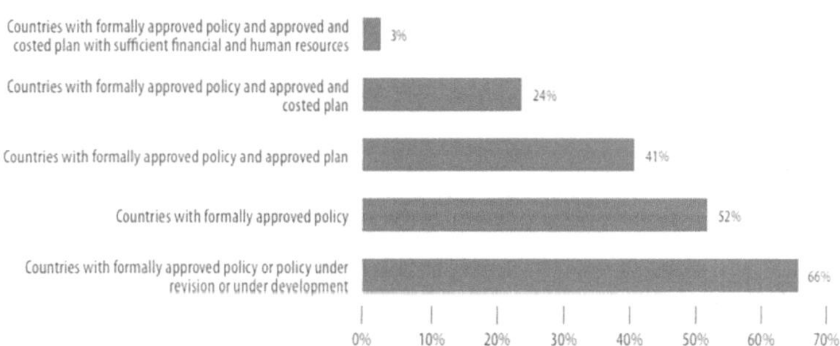

Note: "Sufficient financial and human resources" is defined as having more than 75% of what is needed to implement plans.
Source: GLAAS 2021/2022 country survey.

Estimated annual WASH plan/strategy costs (US$ millions, current)

Great impact could be achieved by making at least one or a few ODF subdistrict or districts systematically, which could trigger self-spreading and scaling up to other areas beyond the district. Similarly, making all efforts to achieve at least one ODF region could motivate officials and staff members in the neighbouring regions to follow suit. This would help them believe that achieving such a goal is not impossible.

Such confidence and belief developed from homegrown examples could strengthen the morale and spirit of the staff and officials of the government and NGOs who are attuned to implementing supply-driven prescriptive approaches to sanitation. It is important to remember that it is a gradual process and can't be introduced and implemented abruptly. Consultations, training and exposure visits helps greatly. Big celebrations and widespread publicity to spread the success of the first few ODF districts and regions are necessary to encourage renewed actions in the non-ODF district and region. All these would contribute to accelerating the pace of achieving ODF national status. During the first decade of CLTS, governments and NGOs were overwhelmed by the ability of local communities to transform their villages into ODF. Following the CLTS approach, hundreds, and often thousands, of ODF villages emerged in countries where the right enabling environment and local support were ensured. However, for various reasons, adequate efforts were not made to replicate and multiply the success of ODF villages in to larger administrative units like blocks, subdistricts, districts, and regions to transform them into ODF. Triggering communities at the village level was not enough to achieve larger ODF areas beyond villages. This is when the real need for institutional triggering was felt.

Institutional triggering tools can help awaken officials and decisionmakers to extrapolate and spread homegrown success within their own districts and regions to eliminate the practice of OD totally. Once achieved, it would certainly accelerate the pace of creating an ODF nation.

8. POOR INTER-INSTITUTIONAL COORDINATION

Often, different agencies working on sanitation and other community development issues have little or no coordination between themselves. The CLTS scaling-up process could be significantly accelerated by engaging a wide range of institutions that play a similar role in improving sanitation. Lead government ministries departments and NGOs working on CLTS may invite and involve other government ministries, departments, and agencies such as education, health, community development, local government, planning, women affairs, agriculture, youth development, etc., to join and add momentum for a national ODF campaign. Other informal yet influential actors include schoolteachers, religious leaders, local political leaders, opinion leader, the print and electronic, the media (press, radio, TV, mobile phone net work etc.), local celebrities, youth leaders, and the like. Institutional triggering is useful to bring these institutions together and help them understand CLTS. The vital roles they can play in scaling up CLTS could add immense value to the process. These are just a few of many ways in which different institutions can be triggered to work together for the elimination of OD from within their areas or jurisdiction of work.

Example: Zambia

CLTS was introduced in Zambia in October 2007 by Kamal Kar when the first meeting of practitioners and donors was held in Lusaka. The Ministry of Local Government and Housing (MLGH), the Ministry of Health (MOH), the Ministry of Education (MOE), WASH NGOs, representatives of major donor agencies, and UNICEF attended this meeting. This seemed unbelievable, and the MLGH representatives expressed their doubts about the claims of achievement and promises of CLTS and its applicability in implementation of CLTS on the ground was left to the MOH and MLGH, who agreed to follow a 'wait and see' approach. However, by 2008, CLTS had scored much success in Zambia, and the other ministries were interested and attracted to pay attention. By 2009, MLGH decided to pay attention and join the CLTS movement. Jointly the MLGH and the MOH started in implementing CLTS on the ground through their district and subdistrict administration. Chief Macha of Choma got especially attracted and was convinced of the power of CLTS in transferring the leadership of the campaign to local communities. With his own initiative Chief Macha continued his work in his Chief dome and soon declared Choma the first ODF district in the country and organised a big celebration with MLGH by the end of 2009. By 2010, MLGH took full leadership to roll out CLTS in Zambia and started co-funding the promotion and scaling-up of CLTS in the entire country in collaboration with MOH, MOE, MDCSS, MOA, MOHA, MOIB, etc. This collaborative approach, involving multiple institutions, proved to be very effective. The government leadership was a major factor which contributed in the success of CLTS in Zambia which was supported by UNICEF's WASH programme, that gained further momentum with funding assistance from DFID, MLGH and partner ministries in scaling up the programme across Zambia. This initiative reached over six million people with the knowledge and importance of improved sanitation and hygiene and has gotten over three million people to build and use improved toilets between 2012 and 2018. The African Development Bank later funded water and sanitation programmes, including CLTS for the tenth and last province directly.

Reported by: Dr. Giveson Zulu (Programme Officer, WASH, UNICEF Lusaka, Zambia)

KEY ISSUES AND CONTEXT FOR INSTITUTIONAL TRIGGERING

In brief, the key issues that institutional triggering aims to address can be grouped under three interlocking and related themes:

- Triggering to improve understanding of CLTS approach amongst key decision-makers
- Ensuring a supportive policy environment
- Encouraging more effective strategies for taking CLTS to scale

These include adjustment and shift in the process of planning, implementation, monitoring, and evaluation of traditional sanitation programme.

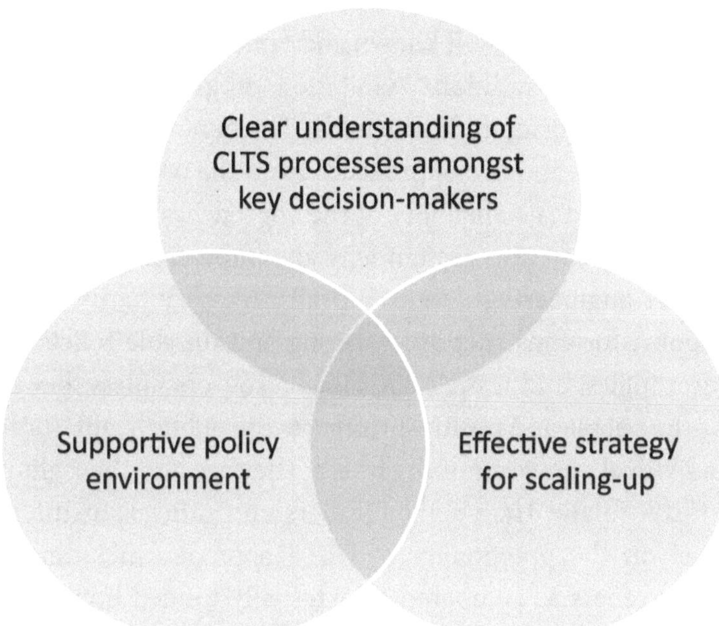

Figure 1: The interlocking elements for successful and outcome focused Institutional Triggering

Institutional triggering works better in situations where many ODF communities emerged through collective local action, yet the entire district, region, or state was not fully ODF. Such examples can work as powerful evidence, which is important for convincing senior stakeholders and decision-makers and other stakeholders. Emergence of a few such examples could be the result of relatively smaller pilot project of the NGOs/government yet to be taken to scale. Institutional triggering aims to address these concerns.

The basic elements required for triggering an entire nation through the institutional triggering process should ideally fulfil the following criteria:

1. The lead ministry implementing sanitation programme in a country should have a few champions convinced and committed to scale up the CLTS approach and are willing to empower the local community to promote collective behaviour change. It

is best to identify champions from amongst the government officials who were well known and famous for their contributions in promoting traditional sanitation programme with hardware sanitation subsidy to households. They are the best person who can compare the two approaches from the perspectives of health outcome and sustainability of the approaches at the level of end-user. They can also explain why any intervention in WASH with proper engineering design and all necessary hardware material support for construction of strong and durable toilets could be meaningless and waste of precious resources unless they are used by the people and positively impacts the public health (both at the individual and community level). They are also the right persons to expose and train senior leaders and officials at the national level on the potentiality of CLTS approach including its cost effectiveness as compared to externally funded household toilet construction campaign without proper training and capacity building on essential behaviour change of the users[29].

2. The lead ministry/agency responsible for sanitation in the country should view sanitation as a cross-cutting, interdisciplinary approach and be willing to involve other ministries and departments to make sanitation a national movement rather than keeping it within their own jurisdiction and control.

Despite the demonstrated success of the CLTS approach in some regions, there could be extremely difficult areas to penetrate and convince communities on the need to abandon the practice of OD due to various reasons. For example, coastal communities living in some areas close to sea in the Philippines and southern Bangladesh, Sierra Leone and a few other countries where high tide sweeps and cleans the faeces deposited by large number of open defecators on the long stretch of sea beach during the low tide twice daily. The beach looks clean apparently after the faeces is washed away by hide tide. The beach gets ready for next batch of open

29 https://www.cltsfoundation.org/benin-gets-its-first-certified-odf-village/

defecators to invade. However, swimming in these beaches are highly unhealthy and could be risky. In some parts of Indonesia there was a traditional practise of defecating in the water. In those areas the women and men used to go up to waist deep streams of water of rivers, springs and/or irrigation channels defecate. As a result, the excreta was neither seen nor it was considered as an environmentally hazardous because the problem of foul odour, flics and insects was absent. However, they continued to contaminate the fresh spring water stream, which flew down the river or the stream and continued to spread the contamination downstream. There are many instances of people defecating on the mountain slopes opposite to their villages and dwelling houses. This way they avoided their immediate problem but were least about the flow of human excreta and the contamination that created hazard for people living in the other side of the mountain slope. Often the deposited excreta gets mixed up with the mountain stream after rain and flows down to villages.

Unfortunately, people living in these areas did not feel the need for abandoning the dangerous practise of OD by investing in toilet construction so long it did not affect them directly.

Involving the highest level of leadership in Madagascar

Chapter 2

Institutional Triggering Methodology

The power of the CLTS methodology lies in empowering the local communities to analyse their own sanitation situation and initiate collective action to stop the practice of open defecation and climb up the sanitation ladder.

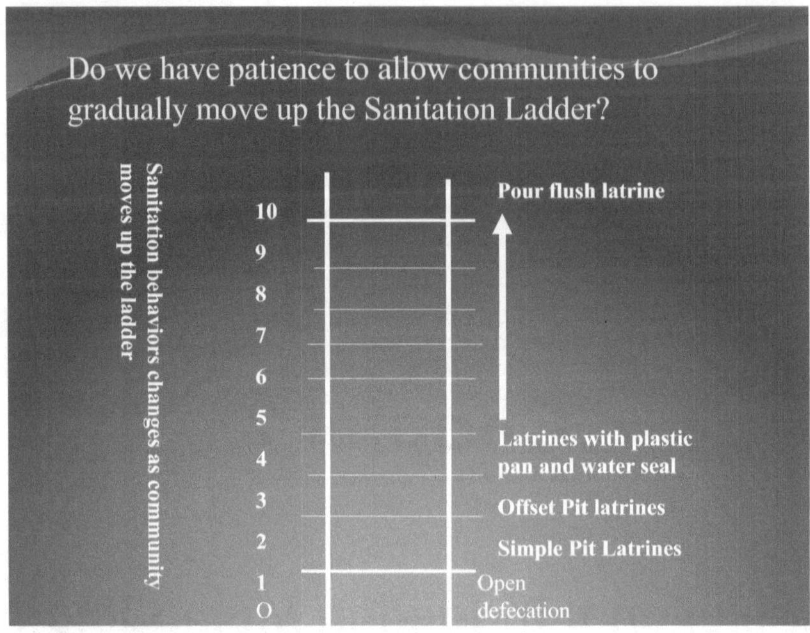

Institutional triggering aims to ensure appropriate action by the responsible institutions to scale up the benefits of CLTS triggering. The methodology for institutional triggering is based on a similar premise to that of community triggering. In other words, it is aimed at evoking a sense of disgust and shame in the community about the current sanitation situation and motivating them to take immediate action. While communities feel disgusted about their own hygiene behaviour specially the practice of OD and decide to construct and use toilets, it is rather embarrassing for the government institutions to realise the reasons for failure of supply driven approach to sanitation being followed by public health, public works, infrastructure, social welfare, and associated departments responsible for maintaining environmental hygiene and sanitation. Often the dismal situation of public toilets compel the people (intended users) to avoid such filthy, smelly and deplorable public sanitation facilities. The institutions entrusted to ensure public health need understand that the reasons for the lack of progress in the sanitation sector is due to their failure to involve the local communities in safe sanitation through total elimination of the practice of OD, hand washing with soap and other essential hygiene behaviour practices in their respective villages, municipalities, blocks, and districts. The message is that total sanitation is not about some people having their safe and clean toilets, but no one in the entire community was violating the basic norms. That it was not about any individual good but a public good must be clearly understood by the community. Due to a lack of community participation waterborne and enteric diseases continue to spread and may affect all irrespective of ownership of toilets.

Generally, the responsibility of the health department of the governments are focused and restricted to curative aspect of treatment but not much for the prophylactic facets and features. However, the number of patients who visit hospitals or outpatient departments of the government hospitals/ health centres for the treatment of diarrhoea, dysentery, cholera, etc. increases the work load of already overburdened hospitals during the peak seasons of monsoon, flooding, drought etc. Further the seasons of festivals and similar other times when most households celebrate with food, drinks, etc., overeating and consumption of unhygienic street food often triggers outbreaks of diarrhoea and other enteric disorders. Due to a lack of awareness of safe hygiene behaviour practices like hand washing before and after food, avoiding uncovered and stale food etc. contamination spreads at a rapid pace during these times. During this time the critical patients visit hospitals, get cured with medication, return to their respective villages and practice OD again. This cycle of getting rid of bacterial contamination causing diarrhoea, followed by hospitalisation and treatment to recover and back to the same old practice, is a vicious cycle. Unless there is a sustained change in hygiene behaviour and a clear understanding of the pathway of contamination, it would be difficult for any government or external agency to stop this completely.

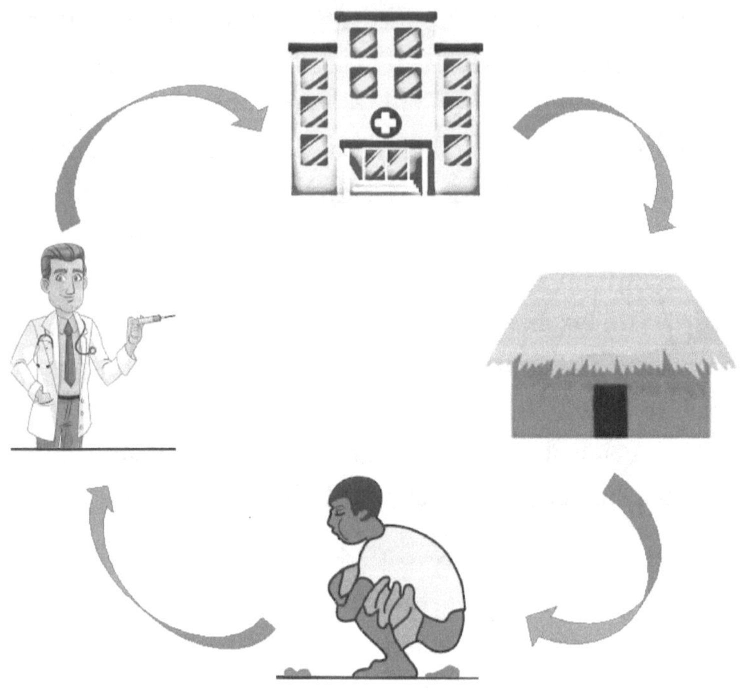

Cycle of recovery from diarrhoea and renewed contamination

WASH is critical to human health and well-being. WASH-related diseases and risks are wide ranging. They include infections transmitted by the faecal–oral route, health impacts from exposure to chemicals and contaminants in drinking-water, and other impacts on overall well-being. In most countries there seems continues to be a continued emphasis more on the curative strategies for disease control, rather than investment in preventative measures. Still, millions[30] of people globally lack adequate access to WASH services and consequently suffer from, or exposed to a multitude of preventable illnesses. Lack of safe WASH negatively affects quality of life and undermines fundamental human rights. Poor WASH services also weaken health systems, threaten health security and heavy stress on country's economy. Inadequate

30 WHO/UNICEF Joint Monitoring Programme (JMP) 2023 update report, Progress on household drinking water, sanitation and hygiene 2000-2022: Special focus on gender.

WASH was attributable to almost 2 million deaths and almost 123 million disability-adjusted life years in 2016 globally[31].

The COVID-19 pandemic has highlighted the critical importance of safe WASH services. WASH services strengthen the resilience of communities, and those are fundamental to the delivery of safe and quality health services to prevent disease outbreaks and to effectively respond when they occur. Two priority areas for government intervention on WASH during the COVID-19 pandemic have been WASH in health care facilities and hand hygiene for all[32].

Institutional triggering does not consist of a single, predetermined set of tools that can be employed for guaranteed success. Each situation requires a unique design of intervention and strategic planning to bring about the desired outcome. However, institutional triggering is broadly a three-stage methodology that is somewhat similar to community triggering, which is administered in a sequential manner. These are as follows:

- **Stage 1: Institutional pre-triggering and preparations**
- **Stage 2: Institutional triggering**
- **Stage 3: Institutional post-triggering follow-up and linkage building**

An institutional triggering exercise requires preplanning, involving a detailed analysis of a country's sanitation scenario and the role of relevant stakeholders, including the government and NGOs. Preparations also involve coordination with key stakeholders, such as senior government officials, policy and decision-makers,

31 State of the World's Sanitation: An urgent call to transform sanitation for better health, environments, economies and societies. New York: United Nations Children's Fund (UNICEF) and the World Health Organization, 2020.

32 Water, sanitation, hygiene and health: a primer for health professionals. Geneva: World Health Organization; 2019 (https:// apps.who.int/iris/handle/10665/330100, accessed 21 October 2022)

ministers, and political leadership. Before starting the triggering exercise, facilitators should spend adequate time to understand the local situation, local people's knowledge, institutional hierarchies, governance architecture, political will and priorities of government policy and the decision-makers. Moreover, it is important to regularly expose senior policymakers, planners, and political leadership to other countries where CLTS has been successfully institutionalised, adopted in the national sanitation policy, and scaled up with significant positive outcome.

WHO ARE THE PARTICIPANTS FOR INSTITUTIONAL TRIGGERING?

The participants for institutional triggering are generally the senior-level officials of relevant institutions, ministries, and government departments in the country, including the administrators and heads of regional and provincial government, whose participation and involvement is crucial in the introduction and roll out of new ideas in the administration. Therefore it is important to choose the participants carefully, who are in right positions to drive national sanitation programmes with others. It should also include officials of similar ranks and authority, from the government ministries and institutions who contribute directly or indirectly in shaping the country's future sanitation status and improving the public health profile.

In most developing countries, such elements of interinstitutional coordination are either weak or missing. Often, the roles and responsibilities of each institution are not clearly defined, particularly when addressing the common objective of making the nation entire ODF. Often, the department responsible for sanitation scores very low in the priority list of departments and ministries so far as the fund allocation in the budget is concerned. Unfortunately, policy and decision-makers, including the political leadership, fail to understand the value of environmental sanitation health and hygiene and their negative impacts on public health. Poor environmental sanitation is reflected in high incidence of diarrhoea, malnutrition, and stunting, which results in weak human resources, perpetuating poverty and poor GDP. Key decision-makers are not always from the WASH/public health ministry or departments alone, but from other ministries like finance, planning etc. who have greater influence in shaping national policy. Therefore, one needs to understand the hierarchy and importance of different ministries in decision-making process of in country. This includes not only the government actors but other institutions such as NGOs/INGOs, Civil Society Organisations (CSO), the private sector, donor agencies, print and electronic media, and religious institutions (temples, churches, madrasas, etc.) involved in sanitation activities.

WHO SHOULD FACILITATE INSTITUTIONAL TRIGGERING?

Successful and dependable facilitators should have a thorough understanding of the CLTS approach as well as good facilitation skills. It is also important that the facilitators have direct experience of working with rural and urban communities to facilitate till the end of the process of achieving ODF status. Additionally, the institutional triggering process in CLTS demands a deeper understanding of the overall context of the sanitation scenario of the country and the reasons for good and poor progress of sanitation in certain areas. They should also be aware of the mechanisms and dynamics of how policy decisions are made, funds are allocated, progress is measured, and roadmaps for achieving targets are drawn. This includes a deeper knowledge of the national sanitation profile, history of sanitation policy and programme development, socioeconomic status, and the country's rank on the Human Development Index (HDI) compared to its Gross Domestic Product (GDP) growth. It is also important to understand the political scenario and the sensitivity of the decision-making framework of the country towards sanitation. The facilitator should have detailed information and background on the policy change of a neighbouring or other country that might have achieved significant progress by adopting an appropriate sanitation policy in the recent years.

The facilitator should essentially possess the skills of moderating dialogue among the higher officials, including ministers, members of parliament alike. The team of institutional triggering facilitators should preferably be led by a lead facilitator or trainer who has years of experience working in the sanitation sector, both within and outside government system. Therefore, a facilitator for institutional triggering should have the right knowledge and skill to connect between the *summit and the base* of country's leadership that can influence the national sanitation context. In other words, it is important that the facilitator be able to link the regional, district, and community level realities with the national context and identify the existing gaps in achieving the desired outcome.

The level of knowledge, experience, expertise and facilitation skill of the facilitator and cofacilitator needs to be decided depending on the requirement, hierarchy and interest of the audience. For example, in the case of an institutional triggering being conducted for high-level officials and elected people's representatives like the Deputy Prime Ministers, Chief Ministers, Governors, Regional Administrators etc., it is important that the facilitator be a very senior and reputed trainer from the respective sector. The facilitator should have adequate experience facilitating high-level meetings with decision-makers, and institutional triggering should not be his or her first exercise as a lead facilitator. The facilitator should have the ability to present a detailed comparative analysis of the sanitation scenarios of the different regions and districts within the country. In their presentation, they should bring a perspective of those areas lagged behind in achieving positive health outcomes through improved sanitation, mainly if it is due to the lack of an enabling environment for scaling up CLTS.

The skills of a good facilitator for institutional triggering lie in his or her ability to draw lessons from successful examples of ODF communities and districts across the country or outside and present them to decision-makers at the national level to trigger actions in support of the growing initiatives from the lower rungs of the administration. Sometimes, the facilitators can bring a group of natural leaders and community consultants from the ODF communities to interact and share experiences directly with the country's senior leadership. Often, such interactions with community members work as an eye-opener for decision-makers and invoke keen interest in them to learn more from the community about the processes by which they achieved success in sanitation. This is important because the right kind of enabling environment and the attitude of letting the community to take lead are the basic requirements for CLTS to succeed. It is in this context that the knowledge and background of the facilitators of higher-level institutional triggering are considered essential. Such forms of 'direct' learning from the country's own communities with its uniqueness and strong local flavour help to convince senior officials about the ability of the community to change their sanitation and hygiene behaviour. Often, the senior leadership of the country do not get opportunities to interact face-to-face with the grassroot communities in an environment that is conducive for the community to express themselves fearlessly. Often, when rural community members are brought to an office or workshop environment in the conference hall for such face to face interaction, they feel uncomfortable expressing themselves freely. Unless this inertia is removed by climate setting and empowering the community members and their leaders, it is difficult to elicit their perceptions of reality in an environment that is alien to them. This should therefore be one of the important responsibilities of the facilitator to create an enabling environment to reverse the learning process. In other words, the members of community should be given the role of trainer and all the others to assume the role of learners (role reversal) with the right attitude of learning from the community.

In short, a lot of skill and a deeper understanding of facilitation are needed for high-level institutional triggering. The facilitator must know how to play his or her cards differently to bring the leaders to a situation where they personally feel motivated to address the plight of sanitation, including the elimination of OD in their own countries, and to do everything needed within their limits. The focus should always be to empower local communities to act without waiting for outside help to solve their own problem. However, the facilitation should not be directed towards accusing or blaming any institution or a government department. Rather it should be appreciating and praising the local communities' success and explaining how the help and support the leadership is essential in multiplying the homegrown success of their own communities to wider areas for the benefit of all.

DURATION OF THE INSTITUTIONAL TRIGGERING PROCESS

As mentioned earlier, the institutional triggering exercise involves the participation of senior leadership in the area under consideration (district, region, or country). Therefore, it is important to keep in mind that the duration of the triggering exercise should be planned in such a way that the participants find it convenient to join. It should not be too long or be organised at a time when the demand for other administrative work is at its peak. It is important to decide the timing of the exercise in consultation with the key officials, without whose active participation the exercise would not be successful.

The institutional triggering activity is divided into three phases:

Institutional Pre-Triggering

This is the planning and preparatory stage for the triggering exercise, which could start a few months before the event and go on up to the day before the triggering actually takes place.

Institutional Triggering

This is the day when the institutional actors are triggered through a set of participatory exercises. Most often, this exercise involves a half-day or a full-day workshop, but in some cases could be extended up to two days.

Institutional Post-Triggering Follow-Up

This is the follow-up stage after the triggering exercise and is an ongoing process until concrete and tangible changes are seen in both policy and programme implementation within the country.

INSTITUTIONAL TRIGGERING AT DIFFERENT LEVELS

Before planning any institutional triggering exercise, it is important to carefully identify the right training institution and the skill sets with which they are it is capable of catering to the training needs of the participants from different levels intending to join. For example, the participants could range from field extension officers to district administrators to senior secretaries of the government, and staff members from NGOs or private sector organisations. Therefore, it is essential to have trainers and facilitators who are capable of imparting training to a wide range of professionals with vast experience from the field to higher policy and decision-making levels. In cases where such knowledge and skill are not available from one group of trainers, a different team of trainers or expert trainers supported by experts. Often senior consultants or academicians from the universities or international institutions may be invited as resource persons may be engaged appropriately.

The triggering cannot be the same for all types of institutions. Institutional triggering for institutions at the district and below differs greatly from the institutional triggering sequences and approach designed for institutions at the subnational level and above. At the same time, it is important to keep in mind that the preparation, design plan, and implementation of institutional triggering for the highest leadership at national level involving Prime Ministers, Deputy Prime Ministers, senior ministers, or even the President are entirely different from the way it is done at the subnational or regional levels.

In the sections below, the objectives and focus of three major levels of institutional triggering have been dealt with in detail, with examples from countries in Africa and Asia.

National Level

EXAMPLE FROM SUDAN

CLTS was introduced in Sudan by Plan International through a hands-on training workshop at the regional-level in 2011. As an outcome of the workshop held in the White Nile state of Sudan, a lot of interest was generated for the adoption of the CLTS approach by the Sudanese states. Plan International and a few of their other partner organisations quickly introduced the approach and rolled it out in their respective programme areas. The best result was found in the Kardofan area of White Nile State. This was possible mainly due to the post-training follow-up support provided by Plan Sudan's field staff. Kardofan fell under the operational area of Plan International Sudan. The success stories of CLTS from the state spread quickly across the country, not only through the NGOs but also through government ministries who had sent their officers for participating in the training workshop in Kardofan. Later in 2017, UNICEF conducted a training workshop on CLTS in Khartoum involving senior officials drawn from all the other states. However, the adoption and spread remained restricted mainly within the White Nile state, with a very encouraging outcome in the reduction of diarrhoea, cholera, and other waterborne diseases. While the practice of OD dropped significantly, handwashing and other improved hygiene behaviours started spreading gradually. In view of the sporadic success in some areas, a national-level institutional triggering workshop was planned by Plan Sudan, involving the government and other major WASH actors. The CLTS Foundation was invited to conduct and facilitate the national-level workshop, which was held in April 2017.

National and state level officials of the government and other NGOs including Plan International participating in a hands-on triggering workshop in Khartoum in 2017.

The minister of health and finance, along with the director generals and heads of departments, actively participated in the workshop and jointly assessed the sanitation scenario of Sudan in a participatory exercise facilitated by the CLTS Foundation. All the participants were divided into four mixed groups. All of them were asked to stay within their respective groups and carryout a particular task given to them. All the members of the group were given a small chit of paper through a participatory process conducted on a massive ground map of Sudan. The officials were asked to stay out and stand around the ground map. They were then asked to move to any state which they thought as the cleanest state of the country. They were asked not to talk to anyone as this was their own individual decision. A movement was noticed on the map. After sometime three groups of people of different size were found to be standing on three different districts on the ground map. While the highest number of people were found to be standing on the White Nile state, a second question was asked to all the participants after a few minutes pause. They were asked to move to a state which they considered as the dirtiest state of Sudan. The participants including ministers and senior officials identified Khartoum state as the filthiest state of the country with the highest percentage of OD and moved there. This finding by senior officials, NGOs, and ministers came as a shock to many, as they found it very hard to believe that the state with the capital city of Sudan emerged as the dirtiest state. But they had to accept the reality as it emerged from their own analysis judgement. Everyone said that the capital city of Khartoum was once regarded as one of the cleanest cities of the world, unfortunately became, the dirtiest city in the country. This finding was the main trigger for a wake-up call to the national planners, decision-makers, and heads of departments responsible for WASH and public health in Sudan. The meeting logically moved into an interactive conversation between the high-level officials at the national and state levels, following which urgent actions were planned.

Subnational/Regional Level

EXAMPLE FROM MAPUTO, MOZAMBIQUE

In Mozambique, efforts were undertaken to address the sanitation policy and its implementation. However, interministerial collaboration in terms of institutionalisation and budget allocation remained a challenge. Therefore, the clear relevance of sanitation in the health and education ministries, among others, was not factored into the national policy. Hence, there was no indicator in the national monitoring system to measure the health outcome as a result of improved sanitation.

In order to address this concern at the subnational level, an institutional triggering exercise was carried out in Zambezia province, which included 21 of the 22 District Administrators (DA) and key actors from the departments of health, education, and agriculture/rural development. The provincial governor of Zambezia province inaugurated and participated in the workshop. The objective of the exercise was to clarify to all stakeholders that sanitation was one of the major agenda items that had the full support and backing of the government. The meeting brought together district administrators, who at the district level played the most important role in decision making and interdepartmental coordination. This institutional triggering exercise aimed to upgrade the level of knowledge and understanding of CLTS among these stakeholders and enhance their commitment to solving the challenges of sanitation in their respective provinces.

H.E Governor of Zambezia province encouraged the participants to involve local communities in making the province free from open defecation.

In the workshop, a major participatory analysis was carried out on a huge paper map (clearly marking the boundaries of those provinces from which either the provincial governors or other senior officials were participating in the workshop) rolled out on the floor to analyse the sanitation situation in their respective administrative jurisdictions. After this exercise, a powerful video recording of a village-triggering event carried out one week before in Quelimani was shown to the administrators. The striking feature of the video recording was the commitment and declaration of a natural leaders who emerged from the triggering exercise who promised to make his/her village ODF within a short time. The outcome of that triggering was like a **matchbox in a gas station.** Later in the week a young villager was invited to the district administrators' workshop in Quelimani, Zambezia, for the presentation of their plan. This event was aimed at reconstructing and staging a 'live' demonstration of triggering with a view to demonstrate the potential of the CLTS approach and the process emergence of natural leaders as agents of change for rapidly improving the sanitation profile of a province. Mr. Januario Jocia, a natural leader who was also a community leader from Mucori B village, presented a vivid summary of the triggering process and the action plan developed by his village community. Workshop participants were intrigued and wanted to know how such great enthusiasm was infused, that triggered the community members to initiate urgent local action to stop the practice of open defecation. Participants were interested in knowing more about the facilitation and other activities involved in triggering the village.

Mapping Exercise at Institutional Triggering workshop at Quelimane, Zambezia District, 23rd April 2018

The participating district administrators keenly observed the process, assimilated the essence of the workshop, and started preparing the outline plan for their respective districts. They prepared their plans based on the following three topics:

- How to make an ODF district
- How to monitor progress towards an ODF district
- Recommendations for enhancing interdepartmental collaboration towards hastening up the process of creating an ODF district

These plans were then synthesised by a group of district administrators drawn from different districts and presented to His Excellency, the Governor of Zambezia province. A detailed plan of action was also developed and presented by the Department.

District Level

EXAMPLE FROM PURSAT PROVINCE, CAMBODIA

Here is a powerful example of the impact of institutional triggering influencing functions of the Provincial Administration from Pursat province in Cambodia. The Deputy Governor of Pursat Province was invited as a special guest in an institutional triggering and capacity-building workshop organised for the participants comprising the heads of districts, NGOs, community leaders and civil society organisations. The idea was to fast-track the process of scaling up CLTS in the province through capacity-building and training organised of officials from different government departments. It was interesting to note that the workshop participants had very little knowledge about the CLTS approach. They didn't know how the approach spread across the entire province and hundreds of ODF communities emerged.

On arrival H.E Ing Kim Leang, the Deputy Governor of Pursat Province, and other high-level officials were greeted by the local community in the workshop. The empowered community members made a very interesting presentations of their analysis of the sanitation profile of their respective villages. The visiting officials were pleasantly surprised to witness such powerful presentations from the community members and their spontaneous initiatives to make their villages ODF. The community members presented detailed plans for their ODF campaign and announced the date after which there would be no open defecation. The community claimed that everybody in the village would be using latrines, which would be constructed during period in every household. The deputy governor was briefed about the CLTS approach and how it triggers communities to stop the practice of open defecation and initiates collective local action to construct toilets at each household using social solidarity and self-help. He also met the natural leaders and community consultants from different areas who participated in the workshop.

H.E. Deputy Governor was so impressed with the initiatives and efforts of the communities that he announced that a part of his annual budget would be made available exclusively for sanitation using CLTS approach. He also stated that he would inform the governor of Pursat Province and others about the strength of CLTS and the need to support the community-led sanitation initiative everywhere.

A. STAGE 1: INSTITUTIONAL PRE-TRIGGERING

As explained earlier, institutional triggering is divided into the following three phases:

1. Institutional pre-triggering
2. Institutional triggering
3. Institutional post-triggering follow-up

In institutional triggering, the first phase of pre-triggering is extremely crucial. This stage is so important that the outcome of IT will depend largely on the quality of activities carried out under the institutional pre-triggering phase. In other words, the outcome and impact of IT will not be very effective unless the pre-triggering activities are meticulously planned and implemented.

Objectives of Institutional Pre-Triggering

- To prepare the base and set the context for facilitating the institutional triggering exercise.
- To prepare the triggering team with relevant information and on the possible challenges might crop up and need to be addressed during triggering.
- To ensure that at least one or two senior officials or ministers are on board during for the triggering exercise. For this, the facilitators need to meet them in advance, explain about the approach its strengths and applicability, and build rapport. In other words, the invited guest should speak about his or her views and experiences about the benefits and applicability of CLTS and the need for its adoption in the regional or national sanitation strategy.
- It is important to ensure that all the materials and logistics required for the triggering exercise are organised well in advance and are in place. The resource person should also be briefed and prepared, and his or her availability should be ensured in the appropriate time slot for triggering.

The institutional pre-triggering phase involves the following preparations that should start well in advance, preferably a month to a few weeks before the event:

1. Identifying participants for the triggering exercise

Sending out invites and ensuring the participation of key people such as heads of local administration, departments or ministries responsible for WASH, NGOs working in the WASH sector, and relevant civil society organisations in the triggering exercise. Care must be taken to include officials from senior levels of bureaucracy who are acquainted with the highest leadership and understand the dynamics between the ministries in prioritising budget allocations and inter-ministerial collaborations. In the case of a national-level institutional triggering exercise, the invitees must also include heads of international, bilateral, or multilateral donor agencies who could share experiences from programmes in different countries. It is always very helpful to include a couple of high-level decision-makers who have had earlier exposure to the triggering process or had visited ODF villages and are convinced about the community's capacity to change.

2. *Collecting information about the geographical and administrative setup of the country*

Relevant information and data should be gathered on the sanitation status of different regions from the ministries and institutions[33] who could contribute directly or indirectly hasten up the process of to achieving the national sanitation goals. This should include data on sanitation coverage and usage, access to basic sanitation, percentage of the population practicing OD, status of health, nutrition including stunting. Rate of diarrhoea, pattern of spread of epidemics like cholera, typhoid, etc., Under Five Mortality Rate (U5MR), Crude Mortality Rate (CMR), Maternal Mortality Rate (MMR), and public health expenditure, including the average annual expenditure for fighting periodic outbreaks and epidemics caused by faecal transmission. The relevant information that should be collected by the facilitator and kept handy for discussions during the institutional triggering exercise are:

---

33 The facilitators should make it a point to involve institutions beyond ministries/ government departments responsible for WASH, such as finance, home, and internal affairs (what percentage of national sanitation budget allocated for sanitation); health (often there is a great imbalance in the investment on curative measures and very little on prophylactic/preventive measures), education (schools, institutional WASH, involving students as agents of change), and tourism.

1. Actor mapping
2. Administrative jurisdiction and boundaries
3. Governance structure
4. Amount of taxes or revenue collected over a period and the percentage allocated for WASH.
5. Budget allocation for sanitation and the chronological pattern of investment and expenditure on sanitation over the last ten years or so
6. Plan and design of the sanitation programmes implemented by government and non-government agencies. To check if the programme is external agency-led, government-directed, or truly community-led.

The team should also try to understand the details of the government's financing mechanism for sanitation, which might involve subsidised or free toilets with prescribed designs or models, cost-sharing of toilets by communities, etc. It is also important to understand to what extent the sanitation policy is focused on generating and sustaining collective behaviour change. The team should also have a broad idea about the outcome of the sanitation programmes—where it went very well and where it did not work so well, and the reasons thereof. During the pre-triggering stage, all preparations for the triggering event should be made[34] in advance.

3. Preparing the leadership of local institutions in advance

The institutional pre-triggering activities include meetings with key leaders or heads of the districts, regional or national-level sector leaders and triggering them to commit to scaling up CLTS if they were not already committed. It is important to have 'one-on-one' meetings with the key officials before the institutional triggering workshop.

34 Such as drawing the map which will be used for the triggering exercise—this is described in detail in the Institutional Triggering section.

It is not advisable to try or trigger a senior official in presence of his or her junior colleagues or subordinates for the first time during the institutional triggering workshop. Senior decision-makers often shy away from making any major commitment if they find themselves in an uncomfortable circumstance in front of their junior staff or ministers. Discussions should be initiated in advance with the senior officials before they are invited to a common meeting or workshop, or else the triggering may not be effective.

This is why institutional pre-triggering is of immense importance, as the outline of the subsequent institutional triggering workshop is discussed frankly in an open forum with everyone's participation. It is easier to get the senior leadership onboard when they have a clear understanding of CLTS and have seen the impact of CLTS on the ground in their own country context.

Steps to follow during Institutional Pre-Triggering

1. Identify the right people from among those in the higher leadership who understand the philosophy and power of the CLTS approach. Arrange separate personal meetings and consultation with them in advance and try to strengthen and fortify his or her understanding and conviction on the efficacy of community-led total sanitation approach. It is important to explain that top-down approach to sanitation in the past did not only crippled and paralyzed the sustainable outcomes of collective behaviour change but failed to invigorate improvement.
2. As the world had seen that hundreds of thousands of toilets were built by the government and other development agencies in the past all over Africa, Asia, Latin America and the Pacific a large majority of those remained as junks dotted all over rural landscape of countries those received free donor funding for sanitation. Those structures were mostly used as store house, livestock shed, chicken coop or purposes other than the

intention for which they were built. Therefore, it is essential to identify the right person in the higher decision-making position, show some of these examples and prepare him or her to initiate proactive role in the process of institutionalising the right approach which is not "outside agency-led" but Community Led.

3. Encourage the selected persons to set a clear goal and a target date for achieving ODF status of their respective district, region, or the full nation and help to prepare a tangible roadmap to scale up CLTS. It must be ensured that the selected person is convinced and assured on the power of CLTS before deciding to join the facilitation team. It is always useful to announce the decisions of such senior people and highlight their commitment during the institutional triggering workshop organised for the field-level staff. This helps greatly in convincing the front line hierarchy.
4. Invite CLTS champions, natural leaders, and officials who created powerful examples of scaling up CLTS in the country as resource persons and to be a part of the institutional triggering team for short time.
5. The lead facilitator should try to have a detailed discussion with the organisers and the concerned people to decide the number of people to be invited for the triggering exercise from the government, NGOs, and civil society organisations. The list of invitiation needs to be prepared meticulously and officially communication should be sent to the participants well in advance by any high official from the department or ministry to ensure maximum participation from all levels.
6. Prepare a list of information (refer to point 2 above) needed during the triggering workshop and request the heads of the districts or regions selected for institutional triggering to come prepared with the relevant data. It is useful to share the final list of participants

of the institutional triggering workshop with others in advance for timely collection of relevant information and data to be shared in the workshop. Periodic reminders may also be sent to the participants to come prepared with the necessary information with the data.

7. Plan strategically to ensure full and active participation of the leaders. Assuming that many of them would not be able to attend the full day's triggering exercise, the workshop may be planned in such a way that the important learning aspects the training workshop are covered or touched upon in the early sessions. In other words the important messages of the workshop needs to be conveyed during the earlier sessions. Keeping this aspect in mind the facilitator should try to design each session as a stand-alone unit of the training and learning event. Whatever activities is carried out in a session, the focus should be on the overall objective of the workshop while each session's objective is met. This is possible if the training is planned and conducted using the principles of the Experiential Learning Cycle (ELC) methodology. It is important to brief the chief guest, invited speakers and the keynote speaker at the the inaugural session on the objectives, and expected outcomes of the workshop.
8. The seating arrangement of the training hall should be either in a U-shape with a big space in the middle or round table arrangements with four or five participants around each table.
9. Training materials like flip chart papers, flip chart stands, markers, projector, big screens, dark curtains, audio-visual aids (cordless microphones—at least three) pointing stick, laser light pointer, whistle should be kept ready the day before the commencement of the workshop. The facilitator team should visit the training hall and functioning of all the equipment's the day before the kick-off of the triggering workshop. Apart from these, notebook, pen, handouts and other essential

training learning materials for the participants (Kar 2010), should be kept ready. Transport arrangements for the groups of participants for travelling to different villages need to be ensured for selected days of village visit. Refreshments and plenty of drinking water for the triggering event should be organised well in advance. Decent institutional triggering venue should be identified, and all arrangements be made in such a way that the senior decision-makers, ministers, and officials feel comfortable and relaxed to participate and learn in a conducive environment.

10. Before the institutional triggering event, the facilitation team should prepare a large 'Country Map' (in case of national triggering) or a 'Regional Map or 'District Map" (in case of regional or district triggering) to be used during the triggering workshop. The map can be prepared by stitching large chart papers with masking tape. For example, in a regional triggering exercise in Sudan, at least 50 large chart papers were pasted together to make a map (e.g., 10 ft x 15 ft or more). The map should outline the national boundaries, delineating the major administrative units, e.g., states/regions, districts, and subdistricts, etc., very clearly so that it is visible when rolled out on the floor to everyone present in the hall. This map is used as a very important material throughout the institutional triggering process for facilitating a visual analysis of region/ district wise sanitation status of the country. As mentioned earlier, the map should be very large, outlining the boundaries of different regions, districts, and subdistricts so that it is visible very clearly to everyone. When rolled out on the floor, one or two person representing each states, regions, or districts should be able to walk on the map and stand on the respective state, region, or district they represent.

Map (10' X 15') showing district wise sanitation status of Sudan

For the first time, the senior-most officials of the government of Sudan were surprised to discover that the district of Khartoum was considered by most of the regional and district officials as one of the dirtiest states of the country. This came as a shock to many who knew that the city of Khartoum had a global reputation of being one of the cleanest cities in the world during and after British times.

B. STAGE 2: INSTITUTIONAL TRIGGERING

The most important and essential requirement of initiating a successful IT process are the skills, experience, and understanding of the facilitators. It is always advisable to invite a senior facilitator who is known in the WASH sector and has contributed in human resources development through skill and capacity building in sanitation or other sector. It is always useful to engage a senior person as a lead facilitator in such exercises to convince the senior and elderly heads of districts, regions, departments, etc., who has many years of experience.

An outline of the Institutional Triggering process is given below.

However, facilitating team should be mentally alert and capable of changing or fine-tuning the schedule flexibly as and when required.

Objectives of Institutional Triggering

- To understand the potential of CLTS and its cost-effectiveness in fast-tracking access to total sanitation compared to other approaches being used in the country at any particular point in time.
- Reviewing the national sanitation policy (if any) in order to fast-track universalizing improved hygiene practices (personal and environmental).
- To stimulate a sense of accountability and self-guilt amongst the higher leadership of the government and concerned

institutions for the poor and dismal sanitation status of the country and its impacts on health and livelihood of people especially those living in their respective constituencies.

It is also focused on creating awareness and making the elected people's representatives recognise their commitments, mandates, and responsibilities to the electorates and denial of the opportunity of holistic development due to dismal sanitation scenario.

- To encourage, and motivate, the highest leadership to recognise the urgency and importance of safe sanitation by adopting a community-led approach for sure and sustainable change leading towards overall growth and development of the region.

  This is only possible if the spirit and philosophy of CLTS is internalised. Merely by implementing the methodology mechanically without deeper commitment may not result in lasting change. However, consultations, visits, high-level meetings, workshops, etc. as post institutional triggering follow up are always useful.

- To develop an action plan to ensure the smooth spread and multiplication of successful homegrown community-led sanitation initiatives across the country.

Steps in the Triggering Process

Institutional triggering can be divided into two distinct phases:

Phase A: Triggering the key stakeholders

Phase B: Facilitation of an action plan towards fast-tracking access to sanitation, which may include:

1. Developing a roadmap for achieving ODF nation/state/region/ district

2. Finalising a feasible target date in accordance with the action plan prepared jointly with the major actors
3. Influencing policy change
4. Fixing monitoring indicators:

It is important to keep in mind that the highest authority of a region, province, or state, like the minister or governor, needs to assume the responsibility of spearheading the implementation plan and follow-up action in accordance with the roadmap prepared during the institutional triggering exercise (i.e. post-institutional triggering follow-up).

Institutional triggering is pointless without the emergence of a commonly agreed SMART (Specific, Measurable, Achievable, Realistic, and Time-bound) plan of action and arrangements for the way forward. Even if the institutions are triggered and encouraged during the session or workshop, nothing may happen on the ground unless the participants make specific commitments and prepare their respective plan of actions before leaving the workshop. Without a plan and systematic follow-up schedule the entire triggering exercise could be futile.

Phase A of Institutional Triggering: Tools and Sequence of Application

A number of strategies and tools can be used to trigger institutional actors, which are as follows:

1. Context setting and perception assessment
2. Comparative situation analysis
3. Area mapping for scaling up

Tool 1: Context setting and perception assessment

This tool is used to initiate a discussion and gather collective perception of the participants regarding the best and worst-performing regions in terms of sanitation and hygiene. This analysis of perceptions by the participants about their own performance creates a dynamic of healthy competition between the regions, states, and districts. It highlights the achievements of an efficient and well-performing administrator and his/her team and their failures. There may be a few who do not assume the responsibility seriously but pass it on to their subordinates.

Steps:

- Divide the participants according to the districts or regions they represent
- Distribute pieces of coloured papers to each group of participant. Each group is given two pieces of paper /cards of two different colours. All the papers /cards should be of exactly same size.
- Ask each group to have a discussion amongst themselves within their group and write down the names of the two worst districts/ dirtiest and the two best/cleanest districts in terms of their present sanitation status. The name of each district must be written on separate papers. That means one name on one card. Please mention clearly that the colour of the card on which best performing district's name should be written and the colour to be used for the two worst performing districts. All groups must follow this rule while writing their district of choices.
- Once the groups write down the names of the districts on the paper/ cards provided to them, collect all the papers and fold them three times to make them smaller in size. The papers should be folded in such a way that size wise they all look the same. Then mix small paper chits in a basket.
- Then pick up the cards one by one from the hat and read out the names loudly.
- While the names are read out from the card loudly, the co-facilitator need to write them down the names (in big font) on a chart paper already pasted on a flip chart board.

- If the name of a particular district is mentioned more than once, put another tick mark by the side of the name of that district as many times as it is mentioned.
- When all the paper chits are opened, count the tick marks against each district and write the score of all the districts on a separate flip chart.

From the final result, it becomes very clear that the name of one or a few district emerge more than other district. This happens in case of both the worst and best performing districts which is based on the number of evaluative tick marks given by the participants against them. An exciting discussion follows when all the groups arrive at a consensus agree on the worst and best performing districts in the country based on the district officials own criteria and scoring. After the discussion, the facilitator should conclude by saying that not all districts are at the same level in terms of access to basic sanitation. Never mention which one is good or bad. The idea is not to criticize the poor performing districts but to encourage a healthy competition among the districts to do better.

Initiation of Institutional Triggering Process

The body language and facial expression of the participants who find themselves in the category of poor/worst performers change which shouldn't go unnoticed by the facilitating team. This exercise aims to stimulate emotions, self-reflection and often shame among the relevant institutional actors responsible for sanitation in the districts and regions. Often IT exercise triggers deep desire and commitment to move forward and change the district in to a better-performer. Flaunt or exposure of poor performers in public always triggers their instinct to move out of the shadow as quickly as possible. Although everyone knows about the poor-performing districts, a participatory analysis together with other districts brings the reality to the public domain. The facilitators must be cautious not to push the discussion beyond a certain limit as it might create embarrassment to participants. It is important to remember that the 'moment the realisation of poor performance' by the respective district is felt it triggers an intent desire to shirk off the image of laggard.

This should be looked at as a positive sign and all necessary support maybe assured to promote the unexpressed desire of the participating district officials achieve success. In the process many participants from the poor performing districts and regions may firmly decide silently to take action to change their sanitation situation which they may not necessarily discuss in public.

Tool 2: Comparative situation analysis

Another tool can be used to highlight the different sanitation scenarios and contexts in different parts of the country. Generally distinct variations in the sanitation status are seen in different districts within a region or different parts of the same district. There could be remarkable progress in the positive health outcomes (e.g., reduction in diarrhoea, etc.) and other benefits beyond sanitation such as collective local initiative to fight seasonal hunger/food shortage, in the village (Monga) in some areas of Bangladesh, improved attendance of children in schools, reduction in the number of children and adolescent girls in school, reduced seasonal migration of labours from the village for manual and the emergence of ODF communities as a result of the community led initiative to end the practice open defecation. Paradoxically, there were areas where local communities awaited external assistance for toilet construction and continued to defecate in the open. No consensus to stop open defecation through collective behaviour change was possible in such areas where the community was more interested in receiving subsidy money or free toilet construction materials.

In such cases, the triggering tool should focus on:

1. Exposing the community members, formal and informal opinion leaders to filthy and disgraceful areas in the village and discuss

the impact of such piles of garbage, solid and liquid waste and ask who were responsible for such a situation? Should the community continue to live in such a deplorable environment and wait for external help for toilet construction to arrive?

2. Examples of districts and regions where the CLTS approach was used successfully to overcome such situation and the empowered community never looked back and awaited for external help at the cost of health of their children and women.

Disgraceful situation (I) was characterised by:

- Clear evidence of continued open defecation and faecal-oral contamination
- Frequent suffering of children from diarrhoea and other waterborne diseases.
- Condition of children, particularly under five years of age, suffering from diarrhoea, cholera, typhoid, and other enteric diseases often become fatal due to dehydration and delayed medical attention.
- Highest number of people suffering from diarrhoea and other enteric diseases were found to be crowding at the primary health centres and hospitals which were already overburdened with an increasing number of diarrhoea patients suffering from diarrhoea during peak seasons.
- Demand and sale of medicine for diarrhea and other water borne diseases goes up which sometimes become out of stock during rainy and flooding seasons. Similarly, the number of patients at the local clinician, physician and village quacks shoots up during particular times of the year on regular basis.
- Absenteeism from schools particularly primary schools increase substantially as compared to other times of the year.
- Availability of manual labour for agriculture and other farm work drops

Successful CLTS implementation in the districts and regions are characterised by the following:

- There is no/rare evidence of spread of diarrhoea or cholera in the ODF communities.
- Latrines are constructed and fully used and maintained by all members of the family without depending on external aid or a free supply of sanitary hardware.
- Local empowerment is evidenced clearly with the emergence of natural leaders and community consultants.
- Natural leaders and community consultants have made their own community ODF and triggered their neighbouring communities.
- The local government proactively engaged to multiply and spread the success of ODF communities. Demonstration of an enabling environment is ensured by organising exchange visits and showcasing ODF communities as learning laboratories.

Steps to be followed for organising institutional triggering workshop:

The following steps could be helpful for the facilitators for conducting an institutional triggering workshop. This is just a guideline, which could be modified by the facilitators according to the local situation:

- Announce the name of the village or clusters of villages or districts that have achieved ODF status in recently (months or year).
- Ask the participants to raise their hands if they belong to those ODF villages, districts, subdistricts or regions.
- Invite one or two participants to share their experiences of achieving success and how they could change their own villages to ODF.
- Ask how many NGOs and partner organisations work in the region and who they are.
- Ask about the process they (NGOs) followed in achieving ODF status.

- In places where there was no NGO or outside support, ask whether the faecal-oral contamination in the neighbouring non-ODF villages was still going on. Who should be held responsible for the continued suffering in those neighbouring villages? Why did the example of a successful community-led initiative to stop the practice of OD did not spread to the adjacent villages? What do they think are the reasons? Who should be held responsible for the failure of local spread and scaling-up of the community-led collective local action to eliminate the practice of OD? Did the people of neighbouring villages were happy and not bothered to live in filthy and unsafe environment? Were they not aware of the danger and risk of faecal-oral contamination due to OD?
- Ask who is responsible for the continued suffering and death of children in the area. If so, what stopped the ODF community from spreading the message of CLTS all over the region for the benefit of hundreds of non-ODF villages?

Tool 3: Area mapping for scaling up

An area or a territory mapping exercise can be used to locate the ODF and non-ODF communities within the districts or regions. This tool visually illustrates the varying progress made by different districts. Through this exercise the administrative heads of the poor-performing districts and regions realise often for the first time a sense of responsibility and their failure of steering their own district to achieve ODF status at par with the neighbouring districts. It is essential that the heads of the local administration of the district or region internalise and understand that the ODF communities achieved their success without any material or financial support from outside other than facilitation for triggering and post-triggering follow-up. This important realisation should be one of the most important element to trigger the administrators and heads of districts. This also provides continued encouragement to better performers to continue their good work and achieve more success.

The following are the objectives of OD area mapping exercise:

- To create a visual display of access to basic sanitation of all the districts and the regions of a country.
- To highlight the areas those successfully made significant progress in scaling up CLTS and spreading the community-led initiative to wider areas involving all the government and the NGOs.
- To identify the districts which either failed to introduce community led approaches or could not scale up the success of their own ODF village. Lack of interest of institutional leadership and/or poor inter-institutional coordination could be one reason among others. The mapping exercise clearly exhibits such variations within a region. This exercise also brings the proactive heads of districts to the forefront, who could extrapolate, mobilise resources and engage the machinery to adopt learnings from ODF villages.
- Mapping exercise also helps in identifying proactive leaders from the subdistricts who made exemplary efforts in successfully scaling up CLTS, for others to emulate from.

Outcomes of the mapping exercise:

1. The mapping exercise offers an opportunity to the heads of the concerned departments to visualise and understand the strong and not so strong performing districts, regions, or states of the country on sanitation coverage. This also allows the leaders to identify and innovative and alternative ways of mobilising resources rather than depending only on the government's sanitation budget. This is demonstrated by some of the proactive heads of administration who scaled up community-led initiatives using unconventional and unspent budget rather than waiting for additional funding support on sanitation.

The ground map immediately triggers action towards improving the sanitation status of the region as it motivates the leadership of the poorly performing communes, blocks, districts, regions, or states at par with the high performers. The regional authorities can also utilise available human strategize to converge, including the transfer of efficient officers, to districts and regions lagging behind in terms of access to sanitation.

Objectives of Institutional Triggering:

1. To understand the potential of CLTS and its cost-effectiveness in fast-tracking access to sanitation through Institutional Triggering.
2. To create a sense of responsibility amongst the higher leadership on the negative impact of poor sanitation on the health and livelihood of people.
3. To motivate, and encourage the highest leadership on the importance of adopting community-led approach for fast tracking overall growth and development of the region, lack of which eventually slows down the overall progress of the country.
4. To develop an action plan to ensure spread and multiplication of successful homegrown community-led sanitation initiatives.

   The map also indicates the distribution of NGOs and other formal and informal institutions rendering support from various sources. It also identifies organisations those operate on minimum funds and hardly receive any external assistance in carrying out their good work. Such analysis on the map helps to harmonise the distribution of resources and institutional support across the region.

   The mapping exercise could very effectively be used in developing a roadmap towards achieving an ODF district or region based on optimal and efficient utilisation of resources by the local administration to ensure that all communities are covered.

Steps involved in facilitating an area/territory mapping exercise:

- The mapping exercise is done in a large hall. All the tables and chairs are removed (or pushed along the walls) to create ample open space in the middle of the training hall prior to the exercise. All participants are asked to stand in a large circle in the middle.

- A big map (only outline boundary) of the region is drawn on the floor by a few participants while the other participants stand around the periphery of the floor map. Participants use chalk, coloured powder, paper strips and other available materials to indicate districts subdistricts in the region and states, or provinces in the country. Often, a large map of the region, district, or the entire country is drawn on a huge sheet of paper (prepared by stitching 15-20 or more flip chart papers with masking tape). This huge paper map should be prepared in advance by the facilitating team. The map is rolled out on the floor and the four corners of the map are pasted on the floor using masking tapes. Alternatively, the map could also be drawn on the floor using chalks and coloured powders (only possible if the floor is not carpeted or made of glossy tiles).
- The heads of the regions, districts, and subdistricts are asked to walk into the map and stand within their boundary of their respective districts. Once they take position on the ground map, the poorly performing districts come in the focus of discussion by the participants (districts identified earlier using the paper chit voting tool) identified earlier (using the paper chit voting tool) come into focus.
- At this stage, cards and markers are given to each head of the region, district, or subdistrict standing on the map, and they are asked to write down the following information on the card given to them:

    - total number of villages in the district
    - percentage of access to basic sanitation
    - number of villages triggered
    - number of ODF villages

- number of NLs and CCs
- scaling-up mechanisms developed, if any

- Once the cards (filled up by the participants with the above information) are placed on the ground, they are asked to walk out and stand along the boundary of the big map. At this stage, the facilitation is handed over to the senior-most/high ranked official of the region or the country present there (the Minister or the Governor or Chief Administrator of the region) to facilitate a discussion amongst the regional and district heads to elicit reasons for such inconsistent progress on sanitation within the same region or province.
- The facilitators at this stage put up a flip chart paper on the flip chart stand and write down the challenges mentioned by the respective administrative heads against the each of the poor-performing district. As the participants mention, the challenges are written on the flip chart in big font so that everybody can see them clearly. Once the list is complete, others are requested to add, modify, or remove any point from the list if they wanted to.
- The potential and innovative mechanisms for scaling up are also noted on another flip chart paper.
- At this stage, the senior-most officer from each district is requested to walk into the map and stand in his or her respective district. A detailed analytical discussion is facilitated amongst the heads of the administrative regions already standing on their respective areas on the ground map.

During this, the facilitator should appreciate the regional and district initiatives. The facilitator should be careful not to embarrass others lagging behind in the process. Such appreciation in front of the whole group is meant to inspire and encourage others who could not do so well. This also motivates the poor performers to openly discuss the challenges and limitations faced by them in their respective region or district in the smooth scaling up of safe sanitation. At this point, it is important to facilitate a way forward discussion amongst the higher officials from the regional or national-level including the ministers present there. Often, the following challenges emerge:

- Problem of clear budget allocation (No exclusive budget is available for sanitation/CLTS) from the national/state level
- Inadequate frontline staff to work on sanitation/CLTS
- Overburdening of field-level extension staff with too many activities and responsibilities not always pertaining to sanitation or CLTS
- Little or no coverage by NGOs, bilateral, or multilateral agencies in some district or region as compared to other districts
- Larger districts or regions with many remote and inaccessible areas coupled with inadequate transportation facilities

Other problems those are often cited are the persistence of the traditional mindset favouring subsidisation or free supply of sanitation hardware and the lack of clear official orders for strict implementation of a 'no-subsidy sanitation policy'. As a result, some NGOs and organisations continue to provide hardware sanitation subsidy at the household level in some areas, which undermines the principles of CLTS. A frank and open consultation often reveals the traditional mindset of a few heads of districts or regions, who prefer to depend solely on government or donor funding for scaling up rather than making efforts to reduce dependence on external funding. It is crucial for the lead facilitator to elicit major learning points from the successful community led/CLTS approaches implemented in some of the districts (pointing to the officials standing on the ground map). The officials from the successful districts are recognised, and given a round of applause. This encourages the poor-performing district and regional administrative heads to learn how to engage natural leaders, community consultants, civil society organisations, and other informal institutions including the religious organisations for successfully scaling-up of community-led initiatives across all sections of society.

Precautions for Institutional Triggering

As in all other social approaches, the methodology of the institutional triggering approach has its own limitations and challenges. The challenges are rather more institutional because this approach requires active participation of the senior-most officials and policymakers of the country in any discussions related to the country's strategy for implementing development programmes. All necessary precautions must be taken beforehand.

Some of the important precautions needed for organising an institutional triggering workshop are as follows:

Selection of participants: The selection of right participants for institutional triggering is very important. Selecting inappropriate participants may not result in the desired outcomes from IT workshops. In the worst-case scenario arrogant participants with inflexible and rigid mindset might spoil the institutional triggering workshop and totally the initiative. It is always better to invest time in carefully selecting IT workshop participants at least for the first few IT training workshops. Participants with prior knowledge about CLTS and familiarity with other participatory approaches may be preferred. A brief resume and background of each aspiring participants may carefully be examined by the lead and co-facilitators before including him/her in the workshop. As it demands a radical change in the traditional mindset, different from someone's year old conviction, lack of good balance of participants (young and old, men and women) may hamper the flexibility of the workshop. In fact, a lot of advance preparations and efforts are needed to organise institutional triggering workshop. Following tips could be useful:

Special logistical arrangements: In all hands-on CLTS training workshops, triggering and facilitating community analysis are the most important segments. Similarly, a thorough triggering exercise is necessary to trigger the district, regional, or national level officials for the purpose of institutionalising CLTS. Therefore a major activity of the institutional triggering workshop is to trigger the senior most officials and decision makers of the country/state on the dire need of adopting a community led approach for tangible health outcome. For this purpose, the entire triggering exercise needs to be done in a conducive environment for the participants, mostly senior government officials and heads of organisations. For this a well equipped air conditioned conference room with all audio visual equipment and comfortable sitting arrangement should be ideal. During the triggering workshop it is advisable to take the participants for a short visit to the field if possible.

In case the senior officials cannot spare time, to visit villages and participate in a 'full-fledged' hand-on triggering exercise, a few members from a couple of triggered communities from within the district or the region are invited to the workshop venue. They are informed in advance to make visual presentation and explain how they changed the sanitation situation of their respective villages following a triggering exercise. They make their presentation using charts and posters (preferably developed during the village triggering). They are also requested to explain as to how they had implemented the community action plan prepared by themselves, and have been implemented. One or two smart and experienced presenters with qualities of natural leader (preferably a man, woman, and a young boy or girl identified as star participants during the village triggering) with loud and clear voice, articulative body language and friendly attitude from the triggered villages are selected by the community to make the presentation at the meeting venue on behalf of the community. They are confident and capable of answering most questions asked by the attending workshop participants. A group of two or three attending members of the community can also participate in the question-and answer session after their presentation.

Often, a rotating presentation is organised at the training venue, where at least two, three or more triggered communities make simultaneous presentation and describe the actions taken on them as follow up to community plan to eradicate the practice of OD and other activities to help move the community up along the sanitation ladder. This includes formation of village and neighbourhood sanitation committees, monitoring mechanisms and protocol for ODF declaration and celebration etc.

Rotating presentations: Keeps all participants actively involved in small group activities and are very effective for individual and group learning. This technique (Rotating presentation) saves time and are very effective as compared to one large group presentation after the other. The community groups also explain possible sources how to procure financial and material support matching with their own contributions, if required. A good presentation always convinces senior officials about the ability of the community to tackle their own problems. Often, the process of institutional support to strengthen community's local collective action begins here. Being convinced and enthused senior officials sometimes make commitment of support and strengthen community's initiative initiated already.

Rotating Presentation

The following list of logistics and training materials are required for the IT workshop:

- A spacious hall.
- Plenty of open space in the centre of the hall where it would be possible to roll out the huge paper map of the entire region or the district (in a Regional Triggering workshop all the districts in the region marked clearly with their respective boundary and in a National Triggering workshop all the regions and the districts are marked) or the whole country on the ground at the centre of the hall as and when required.
- All the chairs and other furniture should be light and easily moveable.
- Plenty of wall space for pasting participating community's maps, charts, posters containing ODF plans, sanitation committees etc., to be brought by at least four communities.
- Adequate time needs to be allowed between the presentations of the two communities.
- Plenty of chart paper and at least four flip chart stands.
- Coloured markers and manila cards.
- Masking tape and scissors.
- It is good to have a long stick or a dried twig or branch of a tree, which could be used as a pointer. Each community group should be given one pointer stick for the use of group presenters.
- Enough markers of three to four different colours of each colour.
- Arrangements to show video clippings of CLTS triggering exercises in villages recorded during field triggering by different groups.
- Other necessary audio visual equipments like cordless microphones etc.
- Big bright screen to display video and slides.

- Overhead projector.
- Standby generator in case of power failure (to avoid loss of time due to power failure).
- Plenty of drinking water, glasses, bottles etc.
- Arrangements for lunch, tea, coffee, and refreshments
- Selected handouts and reading materials may be given to each participant in a folder after the meeting.
- The training hall should preferably be air-conditioned in case it is very hot outside.
- Requests to participants should be made in advance to keep their mobile phones on silent mode in order to avoid interruptions and disturbances.
- Lunchtime could be adjusted so as to cover most important aspects of IT are covered before lunchtime. Therefore every minute of the pre-lunch sessions of the IT workshop should be utilised sincerely.
- Late arrivals and early departures should always be discouraged in subtle ways.
- Selected video clips of live triggering processes with communities, from the country and the neighbouring country should be screened to the participants with arrangements made meticulously in advance.

Workshop sessions: The workshop session should begin exactly on time at the venue as agreed upon jointly by the facilitator team and the organising official in charge of the workshop and be informed to all the participants. If there is a last-minute change in the room number, training hall, etc. in the same venue for any unavoidable reason, the same must be communicated to everyone as soon as possible. It is advisable to put up a poster both at the entrance of the training centre and in front of the earlier venue, clearly mentioning the details of the new location. This will avoid confusion and minimise waste of time.

- The team of facilitators must visit the workshop venue the day before the kick off and check all the arrangements meticulously.
- Power supply, seating arrangements, ambient temperature of the training hall, noise pollution, and other disturbances, etc., must be checked, and appropriate measures should be taken to ensure a high-quality training-learning environment.
- On the day of the workshop, the team of facilitators must reach the workshop venue well in advance, preferably one hour before the kick-off.
- As the participants start arriving at the training venue, they should be welcomed, assisted in registration and may be given important reading materials, notebook, pens, etc. in a folio bag if supplied by the organiser.
- As most of the participants arrive, they should be taken to the refreshment hall for a welcome tea or coffee and snacks. This time can also be used to meet the participants informally and get acquainted with each other.
- The session begins by welcoming the participants and inaugurating the workshop. It is good to invite an important personality to inaugurate the workshop with a brief keynote a speech on the need for such a training workshop and its importance of Institutional Triggering workshop for 'linking the summit and the base' towards strengthening local community's participation in governance and in increasing cooperation between different departments and ministries.
- The chief of the organising committee or the senior most official of the government explains the objective of the IT workshop and introduces the principle facilitator and his or her team members. While introducing them it is important to mention the role played by the facilitators in influencing or transforming the sanitation policies of different countries, highlight their contributions in research, academics, and other areas of

development. This helps the participants to know the trainer or facilitator better and his or her reputation, experience, and other areas of expertise.

- After the welcome address, the formal seating arrangements are changed to a more relaxed and participatory style. The chairs are arranged in a circle or U-shape, leaving a space in the middle or center of the hall. The head table is moved to onc side, and a small table is placed for keeping the projector and other AV equipment and important training documents.
- At the beginning, a game maybe played as an energizer or icebreaker to get the participants to each other better.
- At this stage, the logistics and housekeeping norms (time for tea, lunch, closing, etc.) for the workshop are communicated to the participants. It is important to keep in mind that all the participants may not be comfortable in understanding English language written on a chart. It is therefore important to prepare another set of flip chart written in the language spoken/understood widely in the country. For example; In India more than 300 languages are spoken in different parts of the country. But it is English and Hindi which are widely understood by the people across the country. Similarly, Swahili in Kenya, French in Madagascar and Amharic in Ethiopia are the languages commonly spoken by the people. However, this may not be required for the participants of IT workshop which is participated mostly by the senior officials who are likely to be comfortable with English, French or Portuguese whichever is the official language of the country.
- The overall objective of the workshop is presented to the participants with the help of a slide projector or written on a flip chart. The objectives are written clearly in bold letters on flip charts and are discussed briefly with the participants. At the end of the discussion, the flip chart is pasted on the wall, where it remains for the entire duration of the workshop.

- The workshop gradually start rolling from this point and move towards triggering activities.
- At this stage, video clips of CLTS triggering process in the villages is shown to the participants, and a brief explanation of the different triggering activities are explained.
- It is important to highlight that a hands-on training workshop is different from a traditional training workshop[35].

The trainers should keep in mind that the participants of the workshop constitute senior decision-makers of the government, who have much higher responsibility and administrative power as compared to officials of the same level from non-administrative line departments, e.g., agriculture, irrigation, public works, health, water, sanitation, etc. Therefore, it is very important to maintain the right environment of training for high-level senior officials who should not feel out of place, neglected, or ignored in the training learning environment. This is especially important when the senior officers of one district or province participate with other officials of the same district who are subordinates or assistant officers walking under their administrative jurisdiction. Of course, this does not mean that the senior officers will receive extra attention and priority in the training session. Rather, they would all be treated at par with all other participants in the same workshop. It is up to the experienced trainer as to how he or she would handle the subtle issue of attitudes and superiority complex of some senior officers might have with others without affecting the proceedings of the training. This comes from the long experience of the trainer, which cannot be described in absolute detail. This might vary from context to context, and the strategy to handle them would depend largely on the judgement of the trainer or facilitator.

35 Kar, Kamal (2010) 'Facilitating "Hands-On" Training: Workshops for Community-Led Total Sanitation. A Trainers' Training Guide", WSSCC, Geneva.

Overview of the Institutional Triggering Methodology

Institutional triggering is a methodology developed by the CLTS Foundation which is used at various levels of the government and NGO sectors to accelerate the pace of scaling up of CLTS.

Community-Led Total Sanitation (CLTS) has spread to numerous countries across Africa, Asia, and Latin America since its inception in Bangladesh in 2000. The approach has been widely adopted by governments and organizations working on sanitation and hygiene. Here's a general overview of where CLTS has been implemented:

Africa

CLTS has spread to many African countries, including: • Kenya • Ethiopia • Ghana • Nigeria • Uganda • Zambia • Malawi • Sierra Leone • Liberia • Mozambique • Tanzania • Madagascar

Asia

In Asia, CLTS has been implemented in countries such as: • Bangladesh (where it started) • India • Pakistan • Nepal • Cambodia • Indonesia • Afghanistan • Laos • Myanmar • Philippines

Latin America and the Caribbean

CLTS has also been introduced in a few Latin American countries, though it is less widespread compared to Africa and Asia: • Haiti • Peru • Bolivia • Guatemala

Middle East

A few countries in the Middle East have also embraced the CLTS approach, including: • Yemen

Global Impact

The CLTS movement has been supported by various international organizations such as UNICEF, WaterAid, and Plan International, contributing to its global reach. It focuses on triggering communities to take collective action to stop open defecation and improve sanitation practices.

Institutional triggering is a mechanism to bring about positive attitudinal change amongst institutional actors and inspire them to commit their efforts and political will to supporting CLTS. It involves evoking a strong sense of responsibility among the health professionals for the debility, death, sexual harassment, and financial losses on treatment of cholera, diarrhoea etc. suffered by the poor population, especially the children. This is seen against the backdrop of communities that liberated themselves from unsafe hygiene behaviour and became ODF with minimal facilitation and external support and reduced their disease burden significantly.

CLTS triggering evokes emotions of shame, disgust, and self-respect amongst the community. In institutional triggering, the key elements of change are institutional, professional, and personal in terms of responsibility and commitment to act promptly for the cause. This includes action to empower all communities in a district or region and, giving everyone the opportunity to liberate themselves from open defecation and its consequences through their own collective actions. Much like CLTS triggering, institutional triggering should not be seen as an isolated event. It requires preparatory actions, pre-institutional triggering, institutional triggering, and follow-up which includes post-institutional triggering with appropriate follow-up mechanism. Outcomes are generally aimed at achieving the targets indicated in the plan following a roadmap for a radical transformation that includes a target date for achieving the goal covering a substantial administrative area such as a district, region, or the county. Such action must achieve complete ODF status within the target date. Failing which it might be very difficult and could hardly ever be achieved.

Language: Often, it might so happen that the participants feel more comfortable in a language different from the official language used in the workshop. Often, an English-speaking facilitator faces problem in workshops attended mostly by participants from Francophone and Lusophone countries in Africa and elsewhere. Not necessarily all the Francophone, Lusophone, or Spanish-speaking participants would know English, French, or another language used as the official language of the workshop. Some may understand partly or fully but may not be able to read or write. In order to overcome this challenge, the facilitator should spend at least one full day with the official interpreter/translators assigned for the workshop and prepare him or her for the style of translation to be used to convey the message of the trainer without interrupting the facilitation. It is also important to explain the expectation from the interpreter who has to do a continuous back and forth translation to convey the message of the trainer and the response of the participants back to the trainer.

A translator/s is required for the entire duration of the workshop for continuous language transfer. The workshop organisers must keep in mind that the translator or interpreter will have the dual responsibility of translating the instruction or lecture of the facilitators, the questions, answers, and comments from both the participants and the facilitators. A lot of energy and alertness are needed to manage such intense and deeply engrossing dialogues and multi dimensional communications. It is not physically possible for one person to do all these continuously for more than an hour or so. Therefore, at least two interpreters should be engaged in such intense training workshops. It would also be a good idea to check in advance how many people can speak the official workshop language and are willing to help the facilitator voluntarily by paraphrasing and summarising the content of the discussion as an when required. This could also be checked during or before the commencement of the training.

Schedule: Many a times, senior officials, due to their hectic schedules, leave the workshop and rush to attend other commitments. Such sudden withdrawal from the workshop not only disturbs the proceedings but creates problem in group dynamics and collective learning process by sub groups which they belong to. Hence, late arrival and early departure including frequent absenteeism may become a common phenomenon in some workshops unless adequate notifications are given in advance and commitments for participation are ensured. It should be made clear that such things will not be welcomed. Facilitators should therefore always have an alternative plan in place when senior officials are not in a position to participate. However it is always better to provide repeated reminders to the officials regarding the timing and logistical details of the workshop.

Resource persons: Selectively identifying and inviting champion natural leaders, community consultants, and local officials from the district or region as resource persons for institutional triggering is an effective way of sharing homegrown experience of successful collective local action and scaling-up through institutional triggering. The team of facilitators must spend adequate time preparing these people in advance. Preparation must avoid exaggeration or cooking up stories. It should enable the resource persons to present their own successes, challenges, and innovations in a lucid manner.

Phase B of Institutional Triggering: Targets and Roadmap

Once the participants are triggered and collective enthusiasm towards achieving ODF district or region is created, it is further strenghtened and enhanced with the presence of the highest leadership's in the workshop. The higher level decision-makers should be encouraged to set a date for declaring their respective regions or districts ODF within a reasonable time. If possible, they should publicly declare the target date for the ODF declaration of their respective districts to the whole assembly. If dates are set too far in the future, the facilitators should encourage other participants to share their views and feelings about the proposed slow pace of progress and remind them about the danger that the delay might cause by pushing the ODF date too far away. At this stage, it is important to motivate them indirectly until they get encouraged and reconsider their decision and come up with a new, realistic date. Generally, 30 minutes of time is allowed for senior officials to meet their colleagues to have a quick discussion to strategize the modalities of hastening up the workplan and announce revised dates for the ODF declaration. The planned dates of achievement of ODF by the districts are written on a VIPP card and placed against the respective districts and regions. The administrative heads return to the map to announce the names of their respective districts and regions and the new date of ODF declaration.

During this process, the facilitators should encourage everyone to give a round of applause after the declaration is made by the respective administrative heads. A special word of praise and appreciation is given to those declared early dates for achieving ODF status. Special encouragement should be given to the districts that were performing poorly so far. All such activities are done to encourage the senior officials to own the outcome of the process and involve themselves thoroughly in the way forward actions towards making their respective districts or regions ODF.

Part B of institutional triggering includes facilitation of roadmap preparation and fixing ODF targets as declared by the heads of districts and regions. The facilitator should allow at least one hour for group discussions on this. After the discussion participants are being invited to share in the group their respective roadmap and implementation plan they would work on to achieve within the target dates. Finally the draft ODF action plan should be presented to the large group of interested people.

An ODF action plan should ideally include the following:

- Roles and responsibilities of the officials involved in the implementation of the ODF action plan at different levels should be mentioned clearly. Unless the exercise is facilitated carefully by the heads of department, the chances of disowning such action plan by the concerned officers down the line would be higher.
- The allocation of budgets for each agency/organisation working with the government for scaling up CLTS should be mentioned clearly.
- A comprehensive capacity-building plan for national, regional, and district-level trainers should be developed simultaneously to build their knowledge and skills systematically.

- Establishing appropriate mechanisms for spontaneous scaling-up by engaging natural leaders as community consultants in neighbouring villages and districts is essential.
- Establishing a multi-sectoral and multi-stakeholder institutional platform for coordination and collaboration of efforts and sharing of resources to fast-track the achievement of ODF at the national level has been proved to be very effective.

The ODF action plan and roadmap should be focused on scaling up the successes (even if very small) achieved by the local communities to wider areas. The facilitators should guide the groups and give them input on ways to involve formal and informal institutions, natural leaders, and civil society. Additionally, innovative case studies from other areas featuring the involvement of schools, religious institutions, self-help groups, dairy and agricultural cooperatives, farmer's organisations, market committees, transport unions and federations, and so on, could be shared. These should be used as examples to trigger innovative and region-specific discussions. Appropriate monitoring mechanisms for tracking the progress of ODF districts and regions should also be discussed and incorporated into each district plan.

An outline of the developed plan developed should be presented to the higher leadership at the workshop. It is important to ensure that the state or national minister is present during this presentation. If required, the timing of the final presentation should be adjusted according to the availability and convenience of the minister or whoever is the invited guest of honour. Presence of a minister or a senior decision-maker at the regional or national level is important. This face to face discussion and consultation is very helpful which provides opportunity to the district officials to appeal for support to higher authorities and preferably get some assurance or commitment from them.

Outcomes: As mentioned earlier Institutional Triggering exercises are always outcome focused. As in CLTS triggering the outcome is the emergence of an ODF action plan to be achieved within a stipulated time agreed by the community, the village leadership and members of the facilitation team.

1. ODF roadmap

The ODF roadmap is a well thought-out set of activities that stretches out all the preparations and follow-up actions required to achieve ODF status within the targeted time. As any road leads to a particular destination, passing through different landmarks and milestones, the ODF roadmap should also have clearly defined goals that would ensure desired progress for reaching the target well within the planned period. Without a clearly defined community's roadmap, conceived, prepared, and owned by the community themselves. It is difficult to imagine that the community achieving ODF status within the shortest possible time. Needless to mention here that the quality and pace of implementation of a roadmap is different when the community participate and implement somebody and roadmap in which they had no direct involvement in planning. On the other hand, if a roadmap is prepared by outsiders on behalf of the community, it may not be owned by them, and the externally prepared roadmap might remain as a blueprint document only. Therefore, a roadmap must be made with the full participation of the community which is finally owned by them.

No community in the world would like to continue ingesting each other's faeces for a single day and wait for external support for the construction of toilets. Understanding the naked truth by the community themselves is one of the outcomes of the CLTS triggering process. That is why a truly triggered community will do their best in totally eliminating the practice of open defecation totally and achieve ODF status within the shortest possible time. A roadmap is a very useful tool to accelerate the pace of achieving ODF status within the limits and capabilities of the community concerned. However, it has been seen that some communities achieve ODF status earlier than their planned timeframe. In fact, when the community begins to start constructing their own toilets by stopping the practice of OD, the enthusiasm reaches its peak. Although the community initially thinks that it would be difficult for them to achieve ODF status without external help, their enthusiasm pick up as soon as the collective local action begins, with the natural leaders and community consultants encouraging and helping the households to build their own toilets and abandon the practice of OD for good. Generally, the better-off people construct their own toilets, and some of them extend support to their poor neighbours. Being inspired by the initiatives of the local community, often development agencies, including the government, start supporting them in many ways. Governments realise the fact that saturating villages with toilets in each household is a difficult task as long as it remains an external agency-driven intervention. When the community comes on board and assumes the responsibility and decide to make their village ODF, the intervention of outside agencies are no longer decided unilaterally but jointly with local community where both are equal partners of the decision making process. In other words the participation of the community becomes *interactive* rather than participation for *material incentives.* It is important to remember that the community understands that living in an ODF environment is a dire need required for their own health and safety. Therefore, it is essential that the community realise that they will continue to be in danger of faecal-oral contamination so long the human excreta in the entire village is not safely confined. The spark of energy during the triggering process empowers the insiders to immediately jump into action without waiting for any external help or support. This happens because of the simple realisation that everyone is in danger of ingesting each other's shit as long as one individual continues to defecate in the open. This is the magic *of community-led total sanitation*, which triggers everyone in the community to take action to eliminate open defecation totally.

Often a small section of the community continue to waiting are triggered and ready to build their own toilets. Just don't get worried or too concerned about them. Let them stay and watch the process as it moves on to action planning. Eventually those hardcore subsidy/assistance seekers get influenced by the majority's decision and action towards toilet building/sharing etc. The few subsidy/free toilet seekers get identified as who want to stop eating each other's shit and start constructing simple pit latrines right then and there. Until the self-mobilised members of the community initiate the process with their bold and powerful decision, the laggards and fence-sitters do not change their mind and join others to stop the practice of OD. No human being would agree to ingest human excreta and wait for government money or subsidies to construct toilets. The Institute of Development Study (IDS) Working Paper 184, entitled 'Subsidy or Self-Respect by Kamal Kar', describes this phenomenon in detail[36]. CLTS stimulates the elements of human dignity and self-respect. The entire process of triggering CLTS in a community or village has been explained at length in the earlier chapters. It is extremely important for the facilitators to remember that the ODF target and an achievable roadmap to reach the target is the essential outcome of the triggering process.

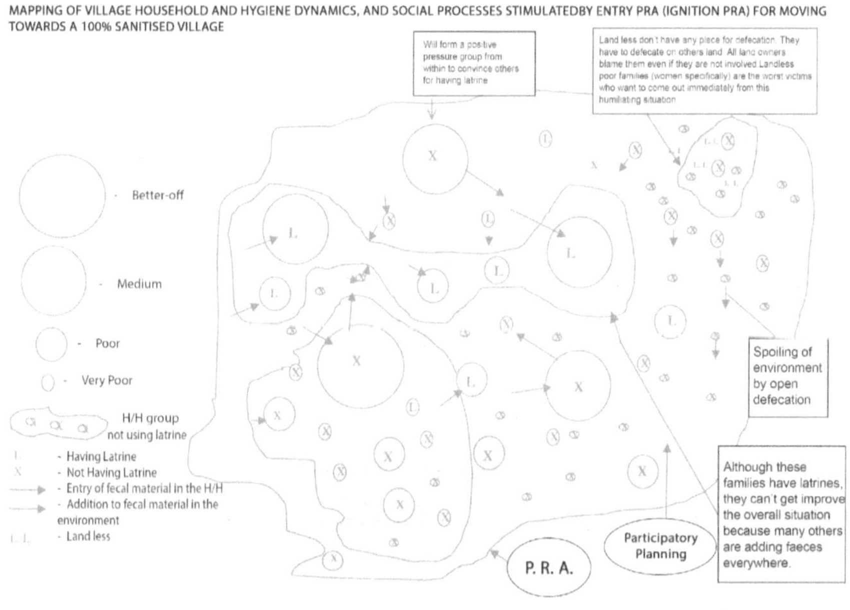

36 Kar, K and Pasteur, P. (2005) 'Subsidy or self-respect? Community- Led Total Sanitation: an update on recent developments', IDS Working Paper 257, Brighton: Institute of Development Studies.

CLTS triggering with the community is not successful unless it inspires the local community to initiate urgent collective local action to stop open defecation and, gradually move towards sustained ODF status. Most triggered communities start digging pits to construct low-cost toilets as an urgent measure to stop the practice of open defecation immediately after triggering. Knowing well that such low-cost latrines would not last long, the communities start planning to improve their homemade, makeshift toilets and gradually move up along the sanitation ladder. Different families starts moving along the sanitation ladder at different rungs of the ladder depending on their capacity to do so. In other words, poor families starting with a basic pit latrine may plan a gradual movement of climbing the sanitation ladder, while the rich and the better-off may opt for an advanced and costlier sanitary option and start moving the ladder from a higher rung. It has been seen in some states in India (Punjab, Himachal Pradesh, and Haryana) that some of the rich families who used to defecate in the open (often in their own land) and never used sanitary latrines over the generations constructed pour-flush latrine as their first ever toilet. Many of these families constructed deluxe or luxury toilets in the family using porcelain pans, floors with mosaic tiles, and expensive facilities for handwashing etc. for the first time as a result of triggering. These families thought that they should not go for simple pit latrines when they had the capacity to spend money and construct comfortable and fancy toilets for the entire family. Many of the families constructed more than one toilet in their compound for use of men, women and children separately. The old traditional mindset of going to open fields for defection in the morning worked as a taboo mostly amongst the older people. They thought that their ancestors used to walk far away from home to defecate and clean themselves in the river or pond and return home with a clean body, bath in the river or pond and pure mind (shuchi). There are many instances globally where some families constructed toilets worth thousands of rupees (hundreds of dollars) leaving behind the practice of open defecation that they were practicing across generations. This meant that lack of money or resources was not the sole problem that blocked them from constructing a permanent and safe sanitary latrine. However, mostly it was the lack of realisation and understanding of the fact that anyone continuing open defecation in the same community or environment would leave all others in danger due to increased chances of faecal-oral contamination. In countries like Bangladesh, India, Kenya, Cambodia, etc., better-off people often supported and helped their poor landless neighbours with space, materials, money, and labour for constructing their toilets. In Indonesia, local dealers of sanitary hardware provided construction materials as interest-free short-term loans. The resource-poor neighbours repaid the cost of material in instalments to their lenders as they received income from the seasonal harvest and sale of rubber and other crops. This happened in the rubber plantation areas of Kalimantan and Sumatra. There are many instances where the neighbours helped in digging pits and constructing toilets for the elderly and differently abled people in the community. Every family tried to help each other to end open defecation totally. These were the bright examples of social solidarity, which happen only when everyone in the village understands the need for collective behaviour change and permanently stops the practice of open defecation.

Facilitating the process of preparing the roadmap is very important from this perspective. Ideally, a roadmap should clearly explain the target date for achieving ODF status.

2. ODF date/target

It is very important to fix a definite date and timeline for the ODF declarations, which is the final outcome of the institutional triggering exercise. In other words, it is meaningless to organise an institutional triggering event unless an outcome focused specific action to eradicate OD is incorporated in the implementation plan of a district or a region. This targeted date would act as a milestone of progress. Such implementation plan emerged through the institutional triggering differs from the style, focus, and objectives of the traditional sanitation programme. For example, conventional municipal and city plans generally use physical indicators for measuring the progress and achievement of the set targets as indicated in the blueprint or plan. For instance how many toilets were constructed, how many public facilities were built, what amount of the budget was spent, and to what extent the work done or accomplished in accordance with the set OVI (Objectively Verifiable Indicators) used in the project log frame.

However, in a participatory plan prepared in consultation with the key decision-makers of institutions and the community, the targeted ODF status includes distinct qualitative changes and improvements together with the physical targets. For example, how many people will use public toilet on a regular basis and what arrangements will be made for repair and maintenance of the facility with full participation of the user community. Public facilities created without the participation of the local community generally end up in unused, defunct, filthy toilets that nobody can use. Often this happens due to a lack of ownership and participation by the local institutions and the community in general. Often facilities are built by higher-level agencies from outside with the expectation that the responsibility of repair and maintenance would rest on the local institutions and the community. This never happens unless the local institutions and the community are involved in the planning process right from the beginning.

There are many instances in the slums of big cities like Kolkata, Mumbai, Nairobi, Manila, Jakarta, etc., where communities manage and maintain public toilet facilities as their own. The users take full charge of the care and maintenance of the facilities created by the government or other agencies. After years of suffering and living in a filthy environment, the community understood the dire need for public toilet facilities for clean and healthy living. In a nutshell, it is bottom-up facilitation that ensures the involvement of the local community and institutions in the planning and implementation of the programme right from the beginning ensuring an interactive participation rather than participation for material incentive. This is contrary to the construction of nice and fancy toilet facilities in a top-down manner without any consultation with the local community. Due to variations in the levels of local participation, the outcomes differ greatly, impacting the overall efficiency of utilisation and cost-benefit of the budget spent on sanitary hardware and construction. Often, the balance of investment in WASH is tilted more towards hardware construction while the behaviour change remains as a low priority area. This occurs mostly because traditional thinking of the WASH professionals which are focused towards engineering design and structural aspects of the new infrastructure created. This may or may not fulfil the preference, conveniences, local culture, taboo and other traditional aspects of the highly diversified communities living in different parts of the world.

Therefore, the externally determined construction of physical infrastructure without the involvement of the local community may not produce a desired outcome hence not be a worthwhile investment. On the other hand, the chances of success are very high for plans prepared in consultation with the local people and implemented with their full participation. Setting up a target in consultation with the end-user community is always more meaningful and justifies the expenditure of the funds spent for the purpose.

There are thousands of examples of unused, defunct toilet facilities all over the developing world. However, the funding agencies and implementers of such projects are happy when the infrastructure is constructed and an allocated budget is spent, which enables them to tick mark check all the indicator boxes against target achievement.

3. ODF action plan

The ODF plan of any village, sub-village, or hamlet must be included in the block, kebele, or commune plan of the area. A block, commune, or fokontany generally has one or many villages. ODF plans for each of these villages need to be prepared by their respective communities before they are included in the block, community, or district plan. Such inclusion of the village plan into the district plan would legitimise the communities' plan and recognise their efforts and guaranteed support from the district/region/state. Recognising the community's plan alone is not enough, but it is essential to extend all technical support and emulate the successful planning and implementation process of the community to all other communities in the blocks, kebeles, communes, and districts. This would hasten up the process of transforming the entire block, kebele, community, or district into ODF. It is unrealistic to imagine that the ODF communities would voluntarily (with their own initiative and expenses) replicate their success of achieving ODF status to different parts of the district. This clearly is a role to be played by the local government and other institutional actors, including NGOs and private sector. Appropriate scaling-up strategies and implementation methodologies need to be developed by the government authorities for smooth scaling-up. Inspite of having many ODF villages, until, if the entire district is not declared ODF. If this situation continues for a substantial period of time, it is clearly an indication of lack of interest, initiative, or failure of the district authorities to replicate their homegrown success in other parts of the district. Often, such things happen when the district authorities and the NGOs promote top-down, free/subsidised, and prescriptive sanitation programmes for constructing toilets in every household. Paradoxically, even if the outside agency constructed, the number of toilets increased but the practise of open defecation continued. It is very important to keep in mind that the construction of toilet and the collective behaviour change are two different aspects responsible for one outcome which is- sustained ODF status. While the former is important the latter is even more important from the stand point of achieving long-term sustainability.

In other words, collective community action and self-mobilisation to stop the practice of open defecation might fail wherever external subsidies and free distribution of sanitary hardware to households continue. It is difficult to imagine both hardware subsidy and spontaneous behaviour change happening together. The one is always contradictory to other.

Efforts to introduce CLTS become counterproductive and are not welcomed by the subsidy-trapped community. Lack of coordination at the district and state level often dampens the community's enthusiasm and zeal to stop open defecation by their own means. The difference between these two approaches are:

1. It ruins the true spirit of collective community participation by alluring free distribution of material incentive.
2. The community prefers to wait for free or subsidised material from the government or NGO for the construction of toilets, which may or may not be used for the purpose for which they are built. Often, these structures end up as a storehouse or chicken coops with hardly any impact in improving the hygiene behaviour.

Preparation of the action plan is the most crucial activity of CLTS, where a community's collective analysis is complete, which transits into the next stage of planning and implementation of the plan on the ground. It is important to mention here that the community's action plan should and must involve as many members of the community as possible, rather than involving a few selected formal and informal leaders.

Lessons: From the above examples, it is important for the development agencies (government and NGOs) to sit down together, discuss, and decide before initiating any action to implement the WASH plan in districts or villages. The roles of each actor must be understood, and all doubts and confusions must be cleared.

4. District and regional monitoring plan

No village or community development plan could be perfect and effective unless it was prepared following the norms and guidelines laid out within the limits of the district or regional master plan. The plan should have the scope and flexibility to mainstream into the larger area plan of the district or state in the future. A village plan developed in isolation and disconnected from the wider area plan is likely to miss out on services and facilities provided by the government and the state, such as proper road connections, electricity, public transport, health and education facilities, communication, market links, livelihoods, solid and liquid waste disposal, and other basic facilities. As a legitimate citizen and a taxpayer of a country, everyone has the right to access the basic services provided by the states.

When a village plan is developed in line with the district or regional planning guidelines, it is likely that the plan will be accepted and incorporated into the district plan. This way, a better functional linkage would be developed between the institutions at different levels for the benefit of the public in general. For this reason, it is essential to include representatives from the local district administration of the area concerned in the planning process.

To ensure the participation of local government, council, district, or block, it is important to send them invitations well in advance and make them aware of the entire planning process. A village plan developed with the local self-government's participation is more practical, realistic, and achievable. Often, a participatory plan with the local government involving other major development agencies like NGOs receives multidimensional support from different partners. These could be financial, material support, institutional, linkage building, etc. Implementation of such multistakeholder projects can ensure much wider community participation and have greater chances of success. Traditionally, the municipal or area plans are prepared based on the available secondary data and information gathered through a questionnaire survey. Most of these data are quantitative in nature and may not adequately capture the qualitative aspect of citizens' responses. Often, the qualitative aspects—like well-being categories, cultural preferences, and variations in choices—differ from community to community. The incorporation of such multidimensional aspects enriches the plan and makes it robust. As 'one size doesn't fit all', incorporation of the micro detail into the plan makes it perfect in meeting the local needs and ensures a greater chance of sustainability.

It is therefore very important to facilitate the process of a district monitoring plan at all levels (village, block, subdistrict, and district) right from the beginning. A properly facilitated plan will capture the local diversity and uniqueness, which would fit very well in the regional or district plan.

How institutional triggering ignited change and made sanitation everyone's concern in Eritrea

Introduction

Eritrea is located in the Horn of Africa, bordering Sudan, Ethiopia, Djibouti, and the Red Sea. It has a population of around 3.5 million[37]. Portable water supply, sanitation, and hygiene coverage are low in general in Eritrea. The government has been working to improve the coverage and adopted a community-led total sanitation approach in late 2008 to completely eliminate the practice of open defecation. Till December 2018, 32% of the total villages in Eritrea declared themselves open defecation-free. Sanitation was considered to fall under the Ministry of Health, and it was realised that there was a need for the local government to play a leading role with technical support from the Ministry of Health. This background provided an appropriate opportunity to organise a national sanitation conference in the capital, Asmara, in December 2018 to raise general awareness of the need for total sanitation.

UNICEF has been a steady partner with the government of Eritrea for almost three decades to strengthen the health sector and ensure clean water and sanitation for all. This conference shed light on the way forward to eliminating open defecation in Eritrea by 2022.

37 https://www.statista.com/statistics/510498/total-population-of-eritrea/.

Institutional Triggering

A National Sanitation Conference was organised on December 11–12, 2018. The conference brought together national, international, and regional experts on water, health, and sanitation and set out the roadmap to ending open defecation in Eritrea. The historic two-day conference brought together over 300 participants, including governors, subregional administrators, and representatives of local government from all six regions. The event was attended by ambassadors and diplomats, heads of UN agencies, and community and religious leaders from across the country.

'Improved sanitation has a great impact not only on health but also on social and economic development, and that is why it is high time that we all work aggressively and collectively to make all our villages and nations open defecation-free by 2022', said Ms. Amina Nur Hussein, the Minister for Health, Eritrea.

Debub region

Debub region is one of the six regions of Eritrea. It is in the southern part of the country. It has a rural population of about 800,000 and 161,371 households administratively. The region is divided into 12 subregions and 216 kebabis, with a total of 1,023 villages. Out of 1,023 villages, 251 villages (25%) have been declared ODF, 115 villages (11%) have been triggered, and 657 villages (64%) have had no CLTS intervention.

What happened after the institutional triggering?

The Community Led Total Sanitation (CLTS) has been implemented in six regions, and the progress varied from region to region. The number of villages where CLTS intervention is not done in the Debub region is more than 50%, as can be seen from the below bar diagram.

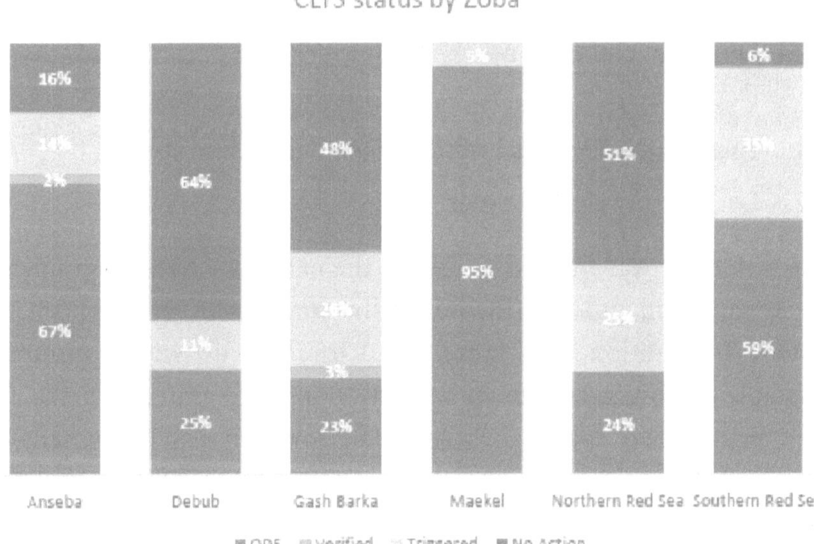

The governor of Debub region, Mr. Ephrem Ghebrekirstos, attended the National Sanitation Conference and stated publicly, 'This conference should have been held before. It is crucial, and all actors have to make sincere efforts to reach the goal by 2022'. He committed that he and his officials were ready to do whatever they could to reach the goal and be ODF.

Right after his return, he held a meeting with all the officials in his region and established a CLTS task force with the following members:

1. Director General of Social Services—Chairperson
2. Head of the Regional Ministry of Health—Secretary
3. Head of Environmental Health
4. Head of the Regional Ministry of Education
5. Head of Zonal Police Office
6. Head of the Commission for Sport and Culture
7. Head of the National Union of Eritrean Women
8. Head of the National Union of Eritrean Youth and Students
9. Director General of the Infrastructural Department
10. Director General of the Land, Water, and Environment Department
11. Head of the People's Front for Democracy and Justice
12. Local Army Commander

The task force was formed to review the existing CLTS programme implementation process, including the monitoring and reporting system. In addition, they were asked to come up with a guiding principle on eliminating open defecation in the region and defining the specific role of each stakeholder. The governor also implemented a quarterly reporting system on the progress of CLTS implementation in the Zoba region.

The governor had organised a total of eight meetings with regional CLTS committees. Two days were dedicated exclusively to CLTS action planning meetings. All these were done within a month of the National Sanitation Conference, where the first institutional triggering exercise took place. In addition, five meetings were held with the sub-Zoba CLTS committee.

The monitoring structure developed in the region is mentioned below:

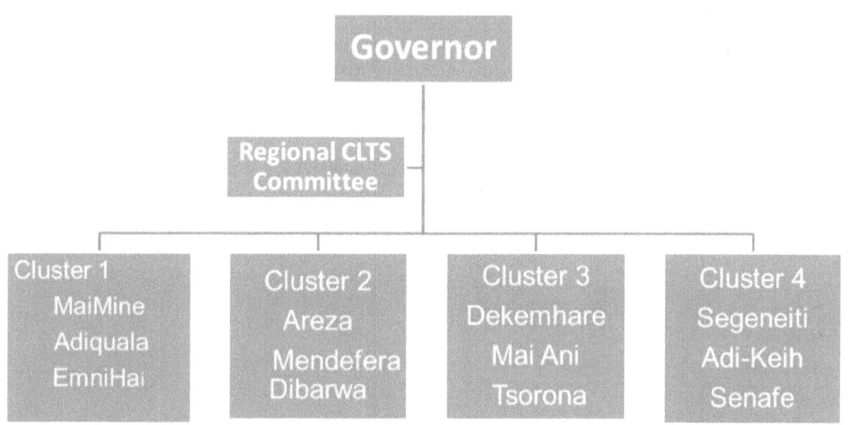

The subregions were grouped into four clusters. The members of the regional CLTS committee divided the clusters among themselves and assumed responsibility. The organisational structure cascaded from the region to subregions through the kebabi administrations to villages.

The local government administrator in each village was given the overall responsibility for intervention and to monitor progress. The Ministry of Health provided technical support through the secretaries of the respective CLTS committees.

Some of the guiding principles developed in the region were:

1. Total elimination of open defecation must be the priority of the region, in line with national policies and priorities.
2. The development of action plans should be based on a thorough review of the CLTS progress in the region and subregions.
3. A three-year time frame must be considered in developing the action plan.
4. A well-designed action plan should have specific targets and indicators to measure progress.
5. The action plan should clearly define the responsibility and accountability of all the stakeholders (institutions).
6. Continuous monitoring for quality assurance must be integrated into the action plan.

Micro planning and review of activities for 12 subregions were carried out.

The review of progress by the regions concluded that in the last 10 years, progress had been very slow. They also mentioned that monitoring CLTS progress should be the task of the Ministry of Health. The monitoring and reporting were weak as the CLTS committee was localised at a subregional level only and had no network at the regional level. Further, there was a shortage of sanitary hardware and other materials. Hence, they restructured the committee and increased the frequency of monitoring and reporting.

> The region decided to declare itself ODF in 2021, which was one year ahead of the national target. The way the process mobilised its people had a great impact on the national ODF roadmap.
>
> **– Yirgalem Solomon, WASH Specialist of UNICEF Eritrea**

C. STAGE 3: INSTITUTIONAL POST-TRIGGERING FOLLOW-UP

Regular and systematic follow-up is required to ensure that the spirit and excitement generated amongst the key actors in sanitation the ministries and other development agencies is sustained. It is important to strengthen interinstitutional collaboration and functional linkages amongst the key actors to address the cross-cutting aspects of national prosperity like to gain through improved sanitation.

The post-institutional triggering follow-up activities should include:

- Distribution of roles (who does what?) to different ministries and agencies interested and willing to participate and assume responsibility and contribute towards achieving ODF national status.
- To avoid duplication of efforts it is essential to distribute roles of different agencies and NGOs to cover all the administrative units of the entire country uniformly. It is important to ensure adequate or special support for neglected and backward regions. Often, most development agencies concentrate their activities in a few regions which are easy to reach, connected by all season roads and other logistic facilities. While the far flung areas with difficult connectivity and logistical inconveniences remain unattended and overlooked[38].
- Actions to formulate appropriate sanitation policies must be initiated with utmost earnest in countries where there is no

38 Chambers, Robert, 1997 Whose Reality Counts - Putting the Last First Intermediate technology Publications London, UK

clearly defined national sanitation policy to ensure an enabling environment and the empowerment of concerned department/s and agencies for faster scaling up of CLTS. In countries where the existing sanitation policy does not clearly define and focus on local empowerment, dialogues to influence and fine-tune the policy are necessary.

- All activities should focus on a joint institutional effort to create a multi-sectoral platform at the national and regional level to scale up CLTS. This platform should have representation from relevant ministries, institutions, NGOs, and civil society organisations involved in country's sanitation sector. Although the cost of scaling up CLTS is far less than the conventional approach of free or subsidy driven toilet construction, the facilitation and post-triggering follow-up costs of CLTS are significant. A common fund with contributions from NGOs, bilateral and multilateral organisations, and the government is always useful for faster scaling up CLTS across the country for which establishment of a common national fund is very useful. In most countries in Africa, more than 80% of the funds for rural sanitation come from bilateral and multilateral organisations (UNICEF, World Bank, UNDP etc.) alone. Often, this funding is targeted at a few selected districts or regions only.

  It is essential that a portion of the government fund from the public exchequer be allocated exclusively for the introduction and scaling-up of CLTS. This would not only establish the national interest of institutionalising community-led approach but would also initiate creation of a dedicated budget for sanitation in the consequent annual plans of the nation. An exclusive unit or section within the secretariat or department for sanitation has been formed in some countries to coordinate all the activities of CLTS across the country.

- Formalising a capacity-building plan is very important area that needs to be addressed during the post-institutional triggering follow-up period. One of the immediate outcomes of an institutional triggering exercise is the interest and enthusiasm shown by the senior officials of the concerned ministries to push the sanitation agenda forward. Many departments or agencies show great interest in receiving hands-on training on the CLTS methodology and learning more about the approach, irrespective of their direct involvement with WASH.

- Depending on the need, different types of training modules may be designed, and a systematic plan of implementation may be made. The training modules will be different for policymakers, mid-level managers, and field-level facilitators. National and regional-level trainers should be involved in conducting these training programmes as much as possible. The capacity-building plan should also focus on developing teams of master trainers and community consultants at the district, regional, and national levels. This would hasten the process of multi-layered scaling-up initiatives. In countries like Madagascar, Pakistan, Bangladesh, etc., Memorandums of Understandings (MoUs) were developed systematically between community consultants and other interested agencies to systematise and streamline the involvement and contribution of community consultants (CCs) in scaling up CLTS. Often, the outcomes of such initiatives are of high quality and cost-effective. ODF villages often become very powerful 'learning laboratories' for continuous capacity-building and training activities at the formal and informal level. Learners clearly understand the CLTS approach and get the opportunity to interact with the ODF communities moving up along the sanitation ladder through the process.

Inter Institutional Review Committee

The formation of an inter-ministerial review committee involving the major institutions engaged in WASH at the national level has been found to be very effective and useful. Example: Madagascar, Mozambique, and Cambodia. The primary objective of this committee should be to review the progress of work by the lead agency, supported by other participating agencies towards achieving ODF national status. Generally, the responsibility of sanitation rests solely on one ministry or department. Often, it is the ministry of water, public works, or public health that looks after sanitation, alongside the primary responsibility of their concerned department. This may not necessarily be very useful in changing the sanitation landscape and expect a rapid progress to occur within a desired timeframe. Sanitation has an overarching implication on the health of the people in general and more particularly in poor dwelling areas like slums and shanties. For instance, a lack of stronger functional linkage or incoordination between the ministry of health and public health or other ministries may create a vacuum or a gap in the control and monitoring of preventable diseases. In most countries, doctors, and health professionals are primarily responsible for the treatment of diarrhoea and enteric diseases who are mostly engaged in hospitals and health centres. Generally, these professionals are not concerned with the prevention or slowing down of the spread of enteric diseases caused due to poor hygiene behaviour of the people living in rural and urban poor areas. These departments are only concerned with treatment when diarrhoea patients are brought to hospitals or health centres. After recovery often the same patient, gets back to his or her village, picks up a fresh infection, and returns to the hospital again. The responsibility of changing the hygiene behaviour of people lies with a different ministry, like public health, community health, etc. Incoordination between these institutions would create gaps and add to the complexities. But if the two institutions work together, there is likely to be a lasting effect on the reduction of diarrhoea and other related diseases. Building interinstitutional coordination and harmony should be the responsibility of both institutions, including the ministry of planning and finance. The chief of the administrative region or the district should also be responsible for strengthening interinstitutional coordination to eradicate the practice of open defecation and other poor hygiene practices. Once it becomes the responsibility of multiple institutions and ministries, the concerned department/ministry responsible for sanitation (WASH) is no longer blamed alone for the failure to check outbreaks or epidemics. On the contrary, other ministries should join them to achieve the national goal of ensuring the good health and wellbeing of people of all age groups.

Generally, the sanitation sector is a low priority area from the ministry of finance for budget allocation. In most countries, the sanitation sector is deprived of a smart and attractive budget allocation as compared to other ministries like water, agriculture, roads, infrastructure, etc. It is important for the planners of the finance ministry to understand that poor sanitation can reduce and slow down the GDP of a country. Even if a nation makes good progress on all aspects of development, a strong nation can never be built with a large population of weak and malnourished children suffering from undernutrition and stunting caused due to poor sanitation. Poor sanitation impacts the economy of the country, affecting tourism, education, industry, sports, and different other aspects. An increasing number of diarrhoea patients in the outdoor sections of hospitals would only add to preventable cost of free/subsidised treatment and maintenance, consuming a lot of staff time and money. It has been seen that such hospitals in ODF areas did not have such an overload of seasonal diarrhoea, cholera, and typhoid patients as they used to have before the introduction of CLTS[39].

Often, some regions or districts make disappointingly slow progress as compared to other regions. Issues like lack of adequate frontline staff, less priority attached to the WASH sector by senior decision-makers, inadequate fund allocation, general lack of sincerity and corruption may become hurdles to making steady progress.

39 Kar, Kamal with Robert Chambers (2008) Handbook on Community-Led Total Sanitation, Brighton London: Institute of Development Studies and Plan UK

The Deputy Minister of Volta region in Ghana with the District Coordinating Executives made commitments to achieve ODF by specific dates in their districts, and eventually an ODF region within six months

Chapter 3

Impact Monitoring of Institutional Triggering

CLTS institutional triggering is an outcome-focused exercise. When triggered properly, the impact is reflected differently at various levels. Hence, its impact should be monitored across all levels, from the national to the subnational to district and down below. The criteria for measuring the impact at each of these levels need to be carefully decided based on the roles of the institutions to be monitored. The sequence of impact monitoring exercises are generally carried out from the higher levels, to institutions at the lower level of the institutional hierarchy. Similarly, the monitoring sequence could be designed in a bottom-up order as well, meaning moving up from the subdistrict to the district through to the regional and national level. The advantages of assessing the impact from below and moving up are many. While assessing the impact from the lower level institution, the monitoring team gains a better understanding of the local perspective and be aware of the situation at the bottom. With these advantages the team could raise and check on many concerns they found at the subnational and district level and raise them with senior policy and decision makers during the impact assessment at the higher level at a later stage.

Many of the challenges and concerns of the lower levels are often overlooked or not clearly understood by the people at the top, who often design and plan, leaving the responsibility of implementation to the officials down below.

The impact monitoring design should primarily be based on the local country context. While developing the multi layered monitoring system, similar examples of the impact of CLTS from neighbouring countries or any other country could be referred to. For example, the institutional triggering exercise carried out by the CLTS Foundation team in 2013 in Abidjan, Ivory Coast, involved five senior ministers, including the ministers of health, finance, foreign affairs, agriculture, and rural development, as well as high officials from the national level. Champions from the concerned ministries of the neighbouring countries of Chad and Benin were also invited as guest speakers and resource persons, mainly for sharing experiences of scaling up CLTS in their respective countries.

As the government and UNICEF officials from Chad and Benin shared their experiences with the workshop participants in Abidjan, it triggered huge enthusiasm and interest amongst the senior government officers and decision-makers to follow their approaches.

HOW TO MONITOR THE IMPACT OF INSTITUTIONAL TRIGGERING

As mentioned earlier, the design and methodology of monitoring the impact of institutional triggering at different levels of institutions are different from each other. The following are some guidelines that could be used as tools and indicators:

At the National Level

- The success stories of the homegrown examples of CLTS in the country or the regions need to be extensively used during the triggering process. These examples could be cited by ministers, national-level leaders, senior bureaucrats, and others during high-level meetings, discussions, workshops, and conferences as and when required.
- Discussions and deliberations to extrapolate the success of the local communities at the highest level of decision-making are crucial. This would pave the way for the formation of appropriate bodies and regulatory authorities to systematise and speed up regional sanitation coverage.
- Monitoring and tracking the progress and understanding the required policy adjustments at the appropriate level are very important.
- Initiatives to prioritise and separate sanitation from the wider domain of WASH must be encouraged. Realising the importance of sanitation some countries formed special directorates or departments for sanitation within the existing ministry of water,

rural development, or public health engineering to prioritise the dire need and importance of sanitation in the national context.

- Interdisciplinary teams of monitors need to be formed. Such impact assessment teams should not be restricted to measuring the output of the programme interventions alone but should look at the health outcomes at the level of the end users or beneficiaries. In other words, the countrywide sanitation facilities and infrastructure created by the government and NGOs to saturate the entire district, state, or region must be monitored in terms of their usage, repair, and maintenance. Often, the sanitation infrastructure created by the government or NGOs are not used fully for the purpose for which they were built.
- Regular monitoring of the progress is essential. Apart from regular monitoring it is also important to look at the direct, indirect and unintended impacts of the interventions. Likewise, it is important to measure the impact of CLTS on the neighbouring communities, districts/states, etc. It is crucial to see the impact of institutional triggering interventions on the local government's policy and practice over a few years and document as to how the WASH programme was being implemented differently after the IT interventions.
- Often, evaluations are focused solely on the major objectives of the programme as mentioned in the log frame and attempt to measure achievements on only the indicated quantitative parameters as mentioned in the OVI. For example, the number of toilets built, amount of external funding, co-funding, local contributions arranged, material cost vs. labour cost and other forms of local participation ratio, etc. Involvement of the local community in the selection of construction sites, toilet design for the convenience of adults, men, women, pregnant women, adolescent girls and children duly respecting other social and cultural preferences of the people, etc. are equally important. Further, the impact monitoring which examines the overall health

outcome of different wellbeing categories of people and throws light to understand them deeply. Therefore, it is important to measure the impact in a phased manner. For example, after five years, ten years, and so on after the implementation.

At the Subnational Level

As organised for the national level, participatory monitoring can be carried out at the subnational level as well, using a similar process. The same big ground map prepared on a very large piece of paper can be preserved and used for the purpose. Such a map is a very useful tool to monitor the progress made by the different districts within the same region. It is always very important to invite the regional governor or administrative head to preside over this participatory meeting/exercises to make it more effective and ensure all post triggering actions by the district and other responsible officials. This provides an opportunity to the senior officials to interact face-to-face with the regional administrator or governor and sort out any administrative or financial issues that might be hindering the process of change using institutional triggering in a particular district/districts. Often, the bilateral or multilateral agencies select a few districts for the implementation of their programmes (including pilot, trails or demonstration) based on their own criteria. As a result, unlike another districts, these selected districts receive funding from NGOs, INGOs, and other agencies in addition to what other districts receive from the government's regular budget. This creates a dichotomy, and is often cited as the reason for slow progress by the nonrecipient districts.

This is where the national and regional government administrations should intervene and invite bilateral, multilateral, and NGOs for consultation and dialogue before selecting the preferred district/s for extending funding support for WASH/sanitation. If the external funding from all sources is distributed uniformly (especially to those districts that lack funding for WASH) involving the government, many unaddressed issues may come to surface which might need joint redressal. For example, vacant positions of field extension staff in some districts often remain a perpetual problem. This could be a macro issue, where the government might have stopped any new recruitment due to the following or more reasons:

- The promotion of field extension staff created vacancies those were never filled up again.
- For obvious reasons women field staff goes on long maternity leave during advance pregnancy and are unable to resume work until the child is six to eight months old. Similarly the paternity leave for men may be considered whenever needed.
- Field staff posted in remote villages always try to get a posting near their hometown or district headquarters for children's education, access to medical facilities, etc.
- With the meagre government salary, often field staff engage themselves in side businesses/enterprises for extra income.
- Keeping regular contact and staying in touch with district or regional officials opens up unexpected opportunities.

In addition to the above, there are reasons which clearly indicate that the initiative and enthusiasm of the field staff are not sustained for longer period of time due to a lack of appreciation, rewards, or an encouraging work environment. Travelling to villages and working alone is often monotonous, mundane, and boring. Since this kind of work is done better in a team, rather than a single individual. In order to overcome this particular situation, field staff in Ghana and Nigeria were advised by the CLTS Foundation to form a follow-up team of three to four people at the village level to work together. The team could include

I. a natural leader,

II. an elected councillor or selected member,

III. the village chief or his representative, and

IV. a representative from civil society like a schoolteacher, village elderly, religious leader, retired government official, ex-military personnel, or an enthusiastic businessman

Whoever is interested to volunteer. If invited, they would all love to join the government initiative to make their village ODF and monitor the progress towards improving sanitation and hygiene status and reducing the incidence of enteric diseases.

At the Individual Level

By thier good work, individuals could contribute a lot and bring about substantial changes. The very nature of triggering is to awaken the minds of people on an activity that benefits many but always originates with the good deed of one or a few individuals. The name triggering indicates a flash of reaction that ignites fire and kick start various activities in a society or living environment. Similarly a triggering activity in CLTS is focused towards creating fire in the minds of people who participates in the triggering exercise. When a few key people from institutions gets triggered in an institutional triggering exercise their conviction on the approach is reflected in the functions and future planning of their respective institutions. Although people from the institutions are triggered, not necessarily the institutional transformation will also start within every institution. However, with a powerful triggering and follow-up, change in the institutional thinking and a systematic transformation begins. As a result of institutional triggering exercise champions can emerge from any level. Though the focus of IT is to transform the general outlook and the approach of institutions in general, often it results in the emergence of new champions. Although these champions belong to a particular institution, they often go beyond the periphery of their organisational boundary and voluntarily start triggering other like-minded individuals across different ministries and institutions. These champions find meaning in their work and the message they wanted to convey for many years through the work of their institutions.

Chief Macha (Choma district, Southern province, Zambia), Ruth Koki Mwanzia (County Minister for Health and Sanitation, Kitui-Kenya), Sr. Domingos (Administrador, Bobonaro District, Timor Leste) who made first ODF districts in their respective countries by institutionalising CLTS.

COMMUNITY AND INSTITUTIONAL TRIGGERING COMPARED

It is important to make a clear distinction between triggering at the community level and at the institutional level. It is also important to note that the definition of ODF is different at the community and institutional levels. While the ODF at the community level means no open defecation, the institutional ODF refers to no institutional open defecation (the word institutional OD has been coined and sarcastically used by the author) means all institution adhering to the principle of collective behaviour change rather than providing upfront free or subsidised sanitary hardware to households and educating them to stop the practice of OD. As mentioned earlier, the abolition of the practice of OD from the community is more a collective hygiene behaviour subject than providing free toilets to each households and asking them to use the same. It is learnt that a top down, prescriptive and external input dependent sanitation approach kills the spontaneity of taking up a collective initiative by the people based on their felt need. This is called "self mobilisation" which replaces the traditional "participation for material incentive". Such an approach did not work in the past decades. The community justifies their ODF status through a host of indicators that include changes in the environment and its impact on the community members. For example, a total absence of faeces around the area, no smell or stink in certain areas of the village those used to be the site of OD, a drastic reduction in the population of flies and other insects that flourish in the OD area, and a drop in the incidence of diarrhoea and waterborne diseases. The hooves of the free-grazing domestic animals, dogs, chickens, etc. do not bring human excreta back home. Girls and women have privacy as they do not have to go in the open to release themselves and enjoy a cleaner and safer environment. There are fewer visits to the doctor by the community due to reduced diarrhoea and other waterborne diseases than before. Everyone, especially children, looks cleaner and healthier with a reduced worm infestation.

In addition to counting the number of ODF villages, the institutions on the other hand set their pointers in the counting ODF districts in the regions. The impact of institutional triggering is reflected in:

- Number of districts with ODF plans within a successfully triggered region, are developed in quick succession by the respective district officials. The implementation of the work plans begins simultaneously at the district level. It is important to mention a word of caution that there could be chances of preparing district plans mechanically without thorough involvement and participation of staff and officials at different level in districts. However, it is important to keep in mind that the acceptance of preparation of district plan in such a participatory way may not so easily be accepted by all. There could be officials who are more used to preparing district plans in a conventional way. In other words, the entire plan is prepared by the higher officials who primarily depends only on hard survey data collected from the field without involving staffs from different tiers in a common forum. Therefore, the plans are generally made on hard statistical data rather than a good mixture of quantitative and qualitative parametres.

- The ODF plans of the districts are shared with the regional headquarters, where the respective date of ODF declaration by the districts is clearly mentioned.
- Districts start to allocate funds from their own budget to make their district ODF rather than depending on the external agency for full funding support.
- The district invite the neighbouring districts and regions to join the ODF celebration together. This spreads the message of successful implementation of institution led collective sanitation campaign.
- Often, the regional head display the monthly monitoring plan for all the districts in the region on a display board in his or her office. The districts making good progress are indicated in green, the medium progress districts as yellow, and the districts with slow and dismal progress as red. The colour changes every month according to the progress made by the districts. This brings every district's progress into the public domain, which often creates healthy competition. In the same fashion, the entire village map of all the households is displayed in a common place in the village after the triggering exercise. The community transfers the ground map onto a huge paper and uses it as a monitoring tool. Whichever household constructs its own toilet and stops the practice of open defecation by all members of the family puts a tick mark on his or her house on the map. Gradually, all the houses on the map are ticked. The

colours of markers change every week to know earlier, middle and late adopters and the total time required for the entire village to become ODF. The same principle is followed to monitor the performance of the districts in the regional office after the regional level institutional triggering.

On the other hand, the communes or clusters of villages must check their ODF status against a number of essential indicators. In conventional sanitation programmes, these indicators are mostly based on the infrastructure created, such as the number of toilets built, physical facilities created, budget spent, amount of sanitation hardware materials distributed, subsidy disbursed, etc. However, this does not always reveal the real picture of an ODF commune or region in terms of the extent of usage of the created infrastructure. Therefore, the indicators must focus on collective behaviour change, including a number of indirect indicators like reduction in the number of patients suffering from diarrhoea and a decline in the spread and number of outbreak of cholera, typhoid, and other waterborne diseases in the area. This can be monitored through the data available at the local health or medical centres and the concerned local government offices. The subsequent impact on household medical expenses and the overall expenditure of the entire community on the treatment of diarrheal diseases could also be monitored through the available data on the sale of medicines and oral rehydration materials.

Another way to understand whether true ODF status has been reached is by assessing the demand and sale of toilet pans and sanitary hardware materials by the local dealer in the nearby markets. The community leaders can keep track of the trend in demand for sanitary hardware. It is important to monitor if the demand for materials for the construction of toilets and other sanitary hardware is increasing or remaining the same after the triggering activities. It must also be noted that the demand for support from government or non-government agencies on sanitation increases after the triggering exercises are carried out. Therefore, it is important for the authorities to monitor the impact of community triggering until a triggered community achieves ODF status.

It is important to ensure that the evaluation of an ODF community, commune, or region is carried out by an independent agency following a neutral verification process after the entire community declares themselves ODF. Once verified and certificated as ODF, the status of the community or commune should be recognised as ODF in the region. Village chiefs of the ODF villages should be felicitated and recognised by the commune chief as an when required. This will create a sense of healthy competition among all the other village chiefs, who will strive to make their areas ODF as soon as possible. For example, in Indonesia, the ODF village chiefs (Kepala Desa) were given caps embossed with 'ODF Village' on them in golden colour. The proud Kepala Desa's wore these caps on special occasions like sub-district and district-level meetings, social gatherings and at other important events. They were recognised for their efforts and inspired other villages chiefs to undertake stronger initiatives to improve the sanitation profile of their respective villages through collective behaviour change and support mechanisms.

It is important to review the impact using indicators that have been finalised through inter-ministerial or interinstitutional consultation. Often, sanitation is the sole responsibility of a particular department or ministry. Apart from the ministry of water generally, other ministries have hardly any link or coordination with the department of sanitation, which is often considered a less important and non-revenue-earning ministry. Often, poor sanitation slows down the progress of a nation in different ways by reducing the GDP growth rate.

In many countries like Mozambique, Cambodia, South Sudan, Benin, Niger, Madagascar, etc., sanitation is usually a subject that comes under the ministry responsible for infrastructure eg., Ministry of Public Works, the Ministry of Rural Development, and the Ministry of Public

Health Engineering, among others. These are focused on developing sanitation facilities and usually follow a top-down approach to address sanitation issues. Therefore, they do not necessarily consider health indicators and lack focus on long-term health outcomes. Often, the lack of coordination with the ministry of health further weakens the monitoring of CLTS implementation and scaling up.

On the other hand, in Kenya, Ethiopia, Indonesia, etc., the ministry of health is responsible for sanitation. However, there is a lack of coordination between the district public health officer and the district health officer. While the former looks into the preventive department, ensuring proper sanitation facilities to avoid the incidence of waterborne diseases, the latter focuses on curative aspects to provide medical support in the event of incidence and spread of such diseases. Lack of coordination between prophylactic and curative departments of health often results in overlooking the preventive aspects of sanitation to reduce the level of faecal oral contamination for the ultimate reduction of patient load in hospitals.

COMMUNITY TRIGGERING AND INSTITUTIONAL TRIGGERING COMPARED

Components of Triggering	Community Triggering	Institutional Triggering
Objective	To trigger local collective community action leading to ODF village.	To trigger collective institutional coordination for collaborating action for scaling-up CLTS towards achieving an ODF region/nation.
Setting/ Environment	In the rural/urban community environment.	In a formal setting (conference hall or a similar place).
Target Audience	Community members including all household members, local leaders, community workers, teachers, health workers, religious/traditional leaders, etc.	Institutional actors from government ministries and non-government organizations including bilateral/ multilateral agencies and donor organizations.
Facilitators	It could be frontline extension staff or district-level officials who have a deeper understanding of local community participation and dynamics including command over local dialects and a flair for interacting with rural/urban communities.	Facilitators have to be fairly senior and experienced professionals on WATSAN with sound knowledge and experience of the functioning of the government department, hierarchy, and protocol. These people should ideally have a reputation as WASH professionals with multidisciplinary knowledge, who should have adequate experience as trainers. The facilitators for this level must have a thorough first-hand experience of CLTS triggering and the follow-up processes up until the ODF declaration.

Prerequisites for Triggering	Rural/urban community where open defecation is practised. (please see pg 14.) 'favourable and unfavourable communities' as mentioned in Handbook on CLTS.	• At least 20–40% of the total villages in the districts are ODF. • Interest and willingness of the district/region/state-level leadership to abolish and transform their regions into ODF • Evidence of failure of top-down subsidized sanitation programme serves as a useful example to justify the need for change in the approach. • Participation of at least a few senior officials who have experienced success in achieving ODF districts/regions through a similar campaign. These people could be the best catalyst to trigger their counterparts and colleagues from other districts and regions by sharing their powerful first hand direct experiences.
Pre-Triggering	• Agreeing on a convenient community site • Agree on the timing and venue of the triggering exercise through discussions/visits with local leaders of the community in advance. • Prepare the facilitating team with relevant data and information regarding the selected community for the triggering exercise. • Gather all the necessary tools and materials for the triggering.	• Meet the high-level leadership of the concerned district/region to ensure that they would lend support to the planned institutional triggering workshop. • Invite the senior leadership to attend the triggering workshop event and deliver a keynote address emphasising the need for abolishing unhygienic sanitation practises. • Try to ensure full participation of the senior-level decision-makers of the ministry, region, and national level with priority. • Prepare the team thoroughly for triggering event.

Triggering	Part A • Use the triggering tools to elicit feelings of disgust, shame, fear, self-respect and emotions until people realize that they are ingesting one another's shit and are eventually triggered to take immediate collective action to stop OD. • Facilitate collective local desire towards ensuring that their own environment is free from OD, which could only be achieved through Collective Behaviour Change (CBC) rather than toilet construction by a few. Part B • Facilitate the community to list names of those who will construct a toilet immediately, repair unused toilets already existing, ensure that every member of the family uses a toilet and those who would share toilets until they build their own. • Communities develop an action plan to achieve the above. • Local natural leaders are identified, who will take the plan forward to achieve the desired outcomes,	Part A • Use a variety of tools and strategies to create feelings of shame, disgust, and a sense of responsibility regarding the lack of initiatives on the part of government officials. It is important to infuse the idea that due to their lack of responsibility, sickness is caused and many people and children were dying. They must assume responsibility to save lives from preventable diseases. • Facilitate a collective agreement amongst the institutional actors to spread CLTS across the nation in recognition of the fact that poor sanitation is *sine qua non* with underdevelopment • Encourage people through facilitation to make them see that there could be more positive outcomes using CLTS, and that it is not a huge challenge and achievable. Part B • Develop a roadmap and target date for achieving the ODF goal (district, region, etc.) • Encourage all participants to express their personal and institutional commitment in public, including forms and kinds of contribution to achieving national ODF status.

Post-triggering follow-up	• Make a plan for follow-up visits immediately following the triggering exercise. Revisit the community soon after the triggering to review the progress and action taken. Regularly return to the community to encourage and support their action plan. • Facilitate development of a community monitoring process. • Facilitate emergence of community engineers and innovators of low-cost appropriate toilets. • Arrange joint verification and certification of ODF villages. • Facilitate ODF celebration involving neighbouring communities. • Move on to post-ODF follow-up activities.	• Strengthen interinstitutional collaboration and functional linkages. • Role distribution of different ministries and agencies interested in participating and contributing towards achieving ODF status • Formalizing the placement and distribution of working area of different agencies, NGOs uniformly across different administrative units (geographical areas). For rendering uniform support everywhere as far as possible.
Natural Leaders	• Emerge during triggering/post-triggering, who drive the communities towards making their village ODF and also ensure that they sustain the ODF status achieved.	• Emergence of institutional champions during the triggering/post-triggering phase to provide leadership towards mobilizing/coordinating resources and making their districts/regions ODF by building interinstitutional linkages and ensuring post-ODF sustainability.

Outcome	• Emergence of natural leaders. • Emergence of ODF villages.	• Well-articulated policy changes that enhance scaling-up of community-led initiatives to achieve ODF districts/regions/nation. • Exchange visits of district, regional, or national level officials to countries where CLTS is being successfully implemented at scale to learn the mechanisms of mainstreaming the approach. • National/regional level planning for larger capacity building initiatives begins with required resources and skilled trainers. • For the first time, fully covered ODF administrative units (subdistrict/district/regions) start emerging.
Role of ODF Community	To sustain the ODF status and move up the sanitation ladder Move towards post-ODF activities such as SLWM. Share and facilitate community's own process of change, innovations, and best practices with other interested communities, Often NLs/CCs trigger other villages spontaneously,	To showcase success for first ODF subdistricts/districts/regions to others interested to follow suit.

Indicators of Change	• Simple pit latrines being built and evidence of 'moving up along the sanitation ladder'. • Sustained hygiene behaviour changes taking place. • CLTS spreading to neighbouring villages. • Beginning of solid and liquid waste management. • Other local initiatives for improving livelihood.	• Stronger functional linkages between ministries, institutions, organizations get established or strengthened • Common platform with funding contribution from different agencies (e.g., national, district-level coalition in Madagascar) is established and is functional. • New department or ministry emerging to address sanitation issues exclusively. • National initiative to change or redesign donor projects already being implemented in the pipeline towards CLTS. • Knowledge hubs to share lessons are established and active. • Interministerial committee is formed to operationalize collaborative actions.
Time taken and flexibility	• Could be done fairly quickly. It is much easier to trigger one community who mostly consider themselves as one undividable whole. There are many commonalities among the households and the families, and the people have a very good understanding and knowledge of the education, sanitation, and well-being profile of their neighbours. People know who defecates in the open and who practises safe sanitation and are concerned about environmental sanitation.	• Institutional triggering takes more time than community triggering mainly because the institutions are more complex and operate at a higher level and handle a lot of diverse issues. Institutions are also governed by a set of rules, norms, and policies set by the national and regional governments. The district administration imposes the rules and regulations and those come from above as government orders. If the

		government's sanitation policy to provide sanitary hardware free of cost or with subsidy; it is difficult to spread the success of ODF villages that emerged from community-led collective action towards stopping open defecation. People with a traditional mindset would prefer to wait for a government dole/subsidy or free money as condition to change their behaviour. This is called "induced participation" or "participation for material incentives". Higher forms of participation—'interactive participation' and self-mobilization—happens only when CLTS is triggered successfully. In such cases, people understand the dire need and urgency of stopping the practise of OD without waiting for the government's help and support. No human being wants to continue ingesting each other's faeces and wait for the government's supply of materials even for a day. CLTS ignites this spontaneous local action with urgency.
Assumptions	While triggering the community, facilitators should always keep in mind that the subject that they are dealing with is real and has immediate relevance/consequences on the lives of the people participating in the activity.	The assumption here is that the participants will do everything that highlights the homegrown success of the community through all government departments and influence the adoption of the process and urgent scaling-up.

Challenges and Limitations	The possible challenges are • Strong culture of subsidy and /or free distribution of sanitary hardware by the government or other institutions working on WASH. • Different approaches to sanitation followed by different institutions working in the same area. For e.g., different rates of subsidy/free distribution/top-down recommendation of different models/different criteria for selection of beneficiaries and many other subsidized schemes other than sanitation. • Lack of interest of the local headman or village chief due to many political associations/vote bank politics, etc.	• Ingrained mentality of the institutional staff that is attuned to implementation of top-down traditional sanitation programmes of prescription, subsidy, and teaching hygiene education. Changing the mindset, attitude, and behaviour of these professionals is a challenge. • Institutionalized corruption and poor quality-control in the construction of sanitary infrastructure and misuse of resources. • Resistance from the technical (engineering) staff to accept the community innovative models of low-cost toilets built with locally available materials. • Difficulty in changing the mindset of the technical staff on the need for collective behaviour change as the first step towards ensuring cent percent utilization of sanitary hardware.
Precautions	A number of precautions need to be taken before community triggering: • Ensure participation of the full community as far as possible. • People from all sections of the society and well-being categories should be present for the triggering exercise of the community.	• Ensure that the decision-makers are convinced about the power and efficacy of CLTS in ensuring a sustainable behaviour change to eradicate the practice of OD permanently across the country. The traditional, top-down, prescriptive, and subsidized mindset of the senior decision-makers

	For example, children, youth and adolescent boys and girls, housewives, mothers, men, the elderly, traditional leaders, the business community, etc., must be represented adequately. • It is important to keep in mind that the perceptions of different categories of people might vary. • In case a cross section of the full community is not represented in the triggering exercise, ideas and perceptions of any one particular category might dominate others' decisions. This might lead to a false consensus and result in an action plan that is never implemented. For instance, the better-off and rich families might say that they all have toilets, hence they are not needed to participate in such a triggering exercise to stop the practice of OD. This triggering exercise unpack the fact that 'so long' some people continue to defecate in the open, no one is safe within the community. Even if some have toilets, they are not free from the danger of faecal-oral contamination which continues through flies, water, wind, grazing cattle, goat and sheep,	must be changed before any large-scale action is initiated on the ground. It is important that sometimes the decision-makers visit communities within their own administrative jurisdiction and see for themselves how the local community could change and improve the sanitation profile of their villages with or without any external help. Vis-à-vis, they should also see some of the unused toilets constructed by outside agencies, which are used as a store, godown, chicken house etc. The practice of OD continues unabated. The conviction of planners and decision-makers on the capacity of the local community to change is of utmost importance for changing the national/regional sanitation policy in favour of CLTS. Often, the national sanitation policy of a country is top-down, which promotes sanitation hardware supply to households. In such cases, promoting CLTS by frontline extension staff is difficult. This is like a 'square peg in a round hole'. Adoption of sustained behaviour change is never possible without an enabling policy environment that supports and empowers everyone in the WASH sector down the administrative line. For example, the highest number of free/subsidized toilets have been constructed by the government in India. However, the percentage

	bicycles tyers, dogs and children's shoes and feet which bring the human excreta comes back to home by these routes. As a result, no one was safe from faecal-oral contamination so long as the entire environment was not ODF. • Ensure that the people from other villages (neighbouring villages) or outside the triggered village do not participate in the ODF planning discussion. In case there are outsiders, they should not be encouraged to offer their ideas and suggestions before the triggered community decides their action plan. This plan must be owned by all insiders. • Outside facilitator must not lead, suggest, or dominate the ODF planning exercise. • Ensure that weak, vulnerable, elderly and differently abled people can participate freely and offer their views and ideas. • It is essential to ensure a relaxed and friendly environment for triggering, where everyone can participate without disturbance or dominance by powerful/influential people who might act as gatekeepers. The time for the triggering exercise should always be decided in consultation with the community	of usage of those toilets by the people has been far below the expectation. In fact, the collective hygiene behaviour change and the construction of toilets must go hand in hand to obtain the most desired health outcome.

	in advance so that they do not face any pressure of time. For example, a village market day may be avoided for the convenience of the rural community. • The facilitators must not promise any financial or material support from outside during or after the triggering exercise. Any indication of donation or subsidy for the construction of household toilets would spoil the spirit of spontaneous participation of a community. Often, such promises by NGOs or external agencies spoil the spirit of CLTS triggering, where the community behave in a different manner to prove that they needed external support in the form of donation or subsidy. They quickly understand the motive and objective of the external organizations facilitating the process. Such community participation for material incentive never triggers self-mobilization. Such participation would never ensure a sustained behaviour change.	

Mr Domingos Martins, District Administrador of Bobonaro pledges to make his district ODF by 2016

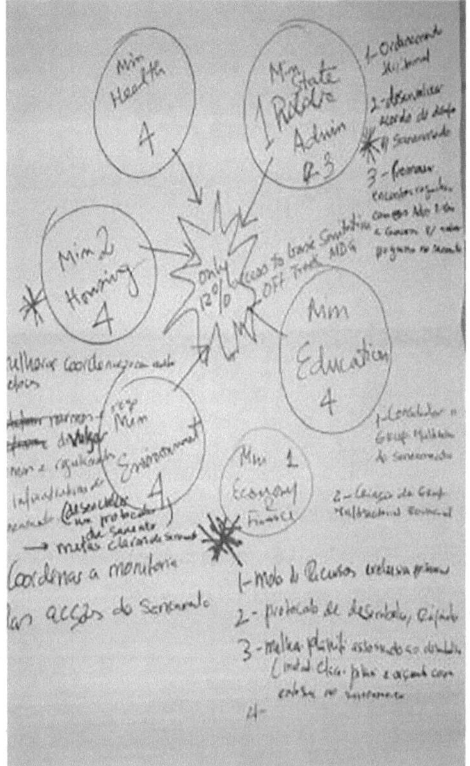

Ministerial representatives analyse present sanitation scenario and suggest three major action points for relevant ministry to improve the sanitation status in Mozambique

National Leaders Championing the cause of eliminating Open Defecation
Deputy Prime Minister and the Secretary of State of Timor Leste championing the cause of country wide roll out of CLTS
Minister of Environment, and Agriculture, Kiribati involving different ministries in scaling up of CLTS

Chapter 4

Recognizing Success

Those familiar with CLTS techniques for community triggering know about the different outcomes associated with institutional triggering (Kar and Chambers, 2008)[40]. There could be different outcomes from institutional triggering not only at different levels but also for different locations of the same level. When triggered properly and post triggering support, is ensured institutional triggering generally convinces senior decision-makers, planners, and administrators on the urgent need to scale up the homegrown success of CLTS across their own region or nation. In other words, being convinced after listening to the success stories of the local community, the national and regional leaders not only start thinking about scaling up the approach to eradicate the practice of OD but also initiate proactive actions in their own constitutions, regions and districts.

However, it could be quite challenging to incorporate the essential elements required to fast-track community-led initiatives within the existing national and regional sanitation policies of the governments. There could be variations in strategies and in implementing the modified policy on the ground. These could be classified into the following three categories:

INSTANT IGNITION OF NATIONAL SPIRIT: BEST OUTCOME

Similar to the *match box in a gas station* in CLTS triggering, one of the best outcomes of institutional triggering is reflected in this category. The major actors in sanitation from within the government and NGOs agree to initiate local action and form an appropriate national, regional, or district-level institutional coalition/platform. This platform leverages the strengths of each institution to scale up the successful homegrown examples of CLTS across the region or country. In some cases, the highest authority of the government (Chief Minister, President, Prime Minister, etc.) may be triggered for

40 Kar, Kamal with Robert Chambers (2008) Handbook on Community-Led Total Sanitation, Brighton London: Institute of Development Studies and Plan UK

countrywide scaling-up of CLTS to accelerate better health, economic growth leading to national prosperity. If triggered effectively, the national leadership might take a deeper look at the sanitation situation and identify the bottlenecks hindering the smooth scaling-up of the success of ODF communities across the nation. The path to achieving the goal could be different, but the targeted objective of an ODF nation remains the same. Some of the activities that hasten the process of faster scaling up are:

1. Critical policy change for sanitation programme implementation. Instead of providing individual household hardware sanitation subsidies and top-down prescriptions of toilet models, it is advisable to adopt a local community empowerment process.

Institutionazation of CLTS in Timor-leste

Almost half the Timor-Leste population does not have access to adequate sanitation, which significantly increases the risk of diseases and malnutrition, particularly for rural households. The 2014 JMP update records access to improved sanitation at 39 per cent nationally (27 per cent rural and 68 per cent urban), with progress flatlining. Sustainability of sanitation has historically been a challenge as traditional approaches of upfront subsidies have negated household and community initiatives and developed expectations of subsidy that have stunted coverage growth. This has resulted in population growth outpacing sanitation provision; a rapid acceleration in sanitation coverage is required for every household to have access by 2030.

There is potential for this acceleration in coverage to be realized. with Dr Kamal Kar's Institutional Triggering of the district administration and community chiefs, along with CLTS implementation in communities, Bobonaro district has realized in less than one year a rapid increase in household toilet coverage.

Other districts are declaring their intention to achieve district-wide ODF status within the year.

NGOs started to introduce the CLTS approach to the sector in Timor-Leste in 2007, which was initially met with scepticism by many stakeholders. Yet by 2012 the national sanitation policy had been approved which recognized the Ministry of Health as the lead ministry for sanitation behaviour change and established CLTS as the lead approach, as by this point the majority of NGOs and external agencies through the Ministry of Health were implementing the CLTS approach for their sanitation programmes. However, CLTS largely remained an NGO-led approach until district-level strategies were developed with the engagement of local government to drive the process forward for district-wide ODF status.

Dr Kar visited Timor-Leste in 2003, and then again in 2013. He visited various communities and met with key sanitation sector stakeholders over three days. During this brief visit it was important to identify the main opinion formers and decision makers within key government institutions, and informally discuss and build rapport with them in a relaxed setting. Through this process it was easier to have an open discussion about what aspects of CLTS were difficult to accept initially and develop a consensus on the way forward. The language around subsidies had to be considered carefully to ensure that a simple debate of subsidy versus no subsidy did not become the focus of decision-makers, but that the complexities of how to best use public finance for sanitation were discussed and understood. The conversation was around shifting from upfront subsidy support to community rewards or incentives for achieving something, thought to be a much more empowering and sustainable process, and ensuring that public finances could be used effectively and sustainably. These ideas were well received.

Through these discussions it was established with the Ministry of public Works that CLTS could be implemented in principle with the addition of the government rewarding communities for making progress and achieving sanitation targets. Dr Kar then shared that CLTS should be a government planned and facilitated approach if it is to have an impact at scale and that the government should use its resources to provide for a collective community reward on verification of ODF status.

Following this, a delegation from Timor-Leste was organized by the CLTS Foundation to visit successful states in India and participate in a CLTS conference. The group on this study tour included key government decision-makers and implementers on sanitation and representatives of the Australian Aid programme, WaterAid, UNICEF, and the Red Cross. This helped the group to gain a broader understanding of CLTS and to grasp the reasons for a change in approach and the benefits to everyone in the group of its successful implementation.

Dr Kar visited Timor-Leste again in 2015 to assist in realizing a district-wide strategy for achieving ODF. He supported the Ministry of Health, the Bobonaro Municipal Administration, the Australian-funded BESIK programme, and other WASH actors to begin a collaboration to end open defecation in Bobonaro district. The remarkable acceleration in sanitation coverage was enabled through a process of Institutional Triggering of the district administration and subsequent cascade down to village leaders, supporting a process of triggering community-wide behaviour change through CLTS from the bottom up, alongside a sanitation behaviour change communications campaign. From July 2015 to March 2016, toilet coverage increased from 47 per cent to 88 per cent. Over 3,300 new toilets have been built and are now being used by householders in Bobonaro, with community members themselves having built all these new toilets so they could stop defecating in the open.

At one of the first community ODF celebrations the district administrator stated; 'Programmes that have focused on sanitation infrastructure, rather than the ending of open defecation behaviour, have made communities in Timor-Leste dependent on material support. But the current approach raises awareness of the impacts of openly defecating to people's health and lives, and motivates people to assume the responsibility of building their own toilet.' The administrator went on to state that in order to sustain ODF status, the local government of Bobonaro would continue to provide support and motivation for the communities to maintain and keep using their toilets. At the first ODF sub-district celebration the Prime Minister of Timor-Leste, Dr Rui M. de Araujo, attended and declared his support for the achievement of the programme and the approach.

As of January 2017, sanitation access coverage in Bobonaro district stood at 95 per cent, with an evaluation of the approach finding on average 67 per cent of final toilets to be of improved status. A robust assessment of the sustainability of CLTS implementation in Timor-Leste found nationally representative slippage rates to be 18 per cent, with approaches now being piloted to address this slippage. Today five districts are nearing ODF, including Liquica, Aileu, and Ainaro, as well as Bobonaro, with another four other districts declaring they also intend to become ODF.

- *Alex Grumbley is a civil engineer and WASH specialist who has been working in Timor-Leste since 2009 with the NGOs WaterAid and plan, and was the WaterAid Country Director in Timor-Leste between 2013 and 2018.*

- *Heather Moran is WASH Behaviour Change Advisor for an Australian government-funded programme in Timor-Leste.*

2. Undertake the necessary administrative changes required to shift from 'top-down programme implementation' to 'facilitation of a bottom-up community-led process' for sustained behaviour change.

Filling in the middle: the Ghana model

CLTS had been introduced in some parts of Ghana at local levels starting in 2007 but, while these activities brought positive results, they did not progress far in terms of increased coverage. At the same time, and unusually, CLTS had been accepted and incorporated in the national sanitation strategy as the only national sanitation approach. Yet a comprehensive plan for how the national policy would be translated into practice did not exist.

The model that was developed identified a central task as 'filling in the middle level' in the district-level administration, as this was the main site of failure in leveraging the experience gained at the community level due to a gap in knowledge about CLTS. The national sanitation strategy was to be rolled out in the 5 (of 10) regions with least access to sanitation by the Ministry of Local Government and Rural Development alongside the Environmental Health and Sanitation Department. The administrative structure is such that regional ministers in each region function as coordination points for all other ministries.

The model involved capacity-building training, planning, and facilitating inter-institutional coordination, including donors such as UNICEF and the World Bank, and NGOs with CLTS experience. Importantly, it also featured Institutional Triggering to stimulate commitment from regional and district-level leadership – regional ministers, regional chief directors, district coordinating executives, and assembly members – to ensure that regional and district-level plans with human resources and fund allocations were harmonized with the national roadmap and plan

(Kar et al., 2015). This strategy then enabled implementation from the top down, driven by the national policy, as well as coordination with Natural Leaders and Community Consultants emerging at community level. The regional and district-level administration was, among other issues, able to convince NGOs at local levels to work with the no-subsidy approach and respect the national sanitation strategy.

3. Conducive sanitation policies in some countries empower local communities to improve their environmental sanitation without waiting for outside help. However, a lack of appropriate policy implementation mechanisms in those countries hinders the smooth rollout of national policy. Appropriate government orders, directives, and regulations for relevant government department and development partner to align themselves and follow the national norms are mandatory. Future investments and funding in sanitation should also be harmonised with the national sanitation policy. The central idea is to ensure that the government takes on the role of facilitator to encourage and support the community-led initiative for total sanitation.
4. Sometimes the policy decision-makers of a nation decisively underplay or discourage upfront household sanitation subsidies until a community achieves total ODF status. This is an intelligent approach to bringing the community upfront as the lead actor. Often, individual household subsidies combined with top-down prescription of toilet models and compulsory hygiene education disable the local communities from acting independently and waiting for external help or support while the practice of OD may continue. Official recognition of ODF communities and clubbing individual household subsidies into collective community rewards often change the entire equation and enhances community

participation. The spirit changes from *'participation for material incentive to self-mobilization'*[41].

5. Once triggered effectively, often the leadership of a region changes the traditional notion of sanitation being the sole responsibility of one ministry (e.g., Ministry of Rural Development, Health, Public Works, Education, etc.). However, it is important to understand that different ministries and departments could greatly accelerate the sanitation movement jointly.

For example, as a result of series of CLTS triggering the President of Kiribati convened a high-level meeting of ministers and bureaucrats after the institutional triggering event organised at Tarawa, which was attended by the President himself and the First Lady. The high-level meeting was also attended by the Ministries of Health, Education, and Public Works, among others. Within two months, a resolution was passed in the parliament of Kiribati to fast-track the sanitation coverage of the entire nation.

H.E. Anote Tong, President of Kiribati accompanied by Ms. Nuzat, Head of UNICEF country office in Kiribati and Mr. Gabriel Rosario, WASH Specialist of the Region based in Suva, Fiji. After a discussion with H.E President he agreed to initiate a nationwide movement to make Kiribati as the first ODF nation in the region using CLTS approach and methodology

41 Pretty, J. (1995) Participatory learning for sustainable agriculture, World Development, 23 (8), 1247–1263.

In another example, as a result of institutional triggering the Chief Minister and Rural Development Ministers of Haryana one of the most progressive state of India realised for the first time that less than 50% of the households used the existing toilets. Whereas the sanitation coverage of the state was more than 86%, which was one of the highest in the nation. Upon this realisation, the honourable CM Mr. Manohar Lal Khattar called the district magistrates of all 21 districts of the state and instructed them to stop any more upfront household hardware subsidies for toilet construction. He requested them to focus on sustained behaviour change to stop the practice of OD. There were instances of well-off people going to defecate in the open with their cars and motorcycles. With the initiative of the Chief Minister and Rural Development minister, the media started spreading the call for ODF Haryana as the state's sanitation campaign, which took the shape of a people's movement. It is important to note that there were many examples of ODF villages created by the triggered local communities without any external subsidy. These led to the landmark decisions of the state government making the essential policy change to fast-track the homegrown success of the local communities across the state. Since sanitation is a state subject in India, the conviction on the power of no subsidy CLTS by the Chief Minister and the RD minister of Haryana was very crucial to change the state sanitation policy. The institutional triggering of the highest leadership was the determining factor that influenced the policy change.

The government of Haryana officially adopts the 'no-subsidy approach'. Thirteen years after the government of Himachal Pradesh decided to stop household subsides for toilet construction, a turning point in the history of sanitation in Haryana occurred when the Chief Minister of Haryana, Shri Manohar Lal Khattar, in presence of all district magistrates declared 'no upfront subsidy' for household toilets under Swachh Bharat Abhiyan. He took the decision after realizing that the use of toilets in the state was less than 50%, when the construction of household toilet coverage under SBA was more than 86%.

In another example, the national sanitation policy of Timor-Leste was changed from individual household subsidy to no-subsidy provision with the intervention of the deputy Prime Minister and other senior ministers.

CONVINCED, YET CONFUSED!

This is a situation where, due to many administrative and bureaucratic complexities and bottlenecks, senior decision-makers at the national level find it difficult to change the sanitation policy. Although policymakers are convinced about the need to eradicate the practice of OD, it is not easy to remove all the hurdles essential to institutionalising the no-subsidy local empowerment approach of CLTS, which includes:

1. Continuation of ongoing latrine construction programmes with upfront sanitation hardware subsidies or free construction of toilets funded by donor agencies. In such situations, it is often difficult to withdraw the supply of free or subsidised sanitary hardware to individual households. Such subsidised hardware-driven programmes deviate from the focus of community-led initiatives to a supply-driven programme, which often results in failure due to non-usage of the toilets by the people for whom they were built. The central purpose of triggering CLTS for evoking a self-mobilised people's campaign was not successful due to continued supply of free sanitation hardware materials from outside.
2. It is difficult to expect collective local action towards behaviour change against OD in such situation. Expectations to receive free sanitation hardware and waiting for the same become a common mindset among the people in the community. This has become a norm over decades of top-down subsidised latrine construction programmes implemented by outside development agencies. Often, an earlier MoU signed between the government of a country and an external donor agency prevents the national government from shifting focus and adopting the homegrown successful examples of ODF communities for scaling up across the nation.
3. Similarly, the government in some countries signed MoUs with outside funding agencies to implement the CLTS approach to improve sanitation even before the approach was learned by WASH professionals in their own countries. Traditionally, many countries in Africa (Uganda, Eswatini (Swaziland)) and Asia were using the PHAST approach under the World Bank and UNICEF supported programmes. It was difficult to introduce and scale up the implementation of CLTS in countries like Uganda, Eswatini etc., where PHAST, SARAR, and other approaches to sanitation with subsidy coupled with top-down teaching of hygiene education were in use for several years. Since those approaches

were packaged and implemented through government machinery under specific programmes with financial and hardware support for the beneficiaries, they were more popular and attractive.

4. It is quite a challenge to implement CLTS where household-level sanitation subsidy culture was predominant. There are programmes in countries where subsidies are being given to local communities for various basic needs, such as free housing, subsidised food grains, free medical treatment, and even the distribution of household goods such as TVs, fridges, motorcycle etc. eg: Tamil Nadu, India and Mozambique.
5. The outcome of institutional triggering depends largely on the enabling environment of the institutions. Institutional triggering is generally less successful where the key institutional actors are reluctant to accept any major change in the modus operandi in the management and operation of the institution. I have often seen that some of the key actors (a few senior officials) do not show up on the day of IT or report very late, despite the promise to participate in the exercise/workshop. Often, in spite of the commitment of serious follow up made by the officials during the IT workshop not much is done proactively after the workshop. In fact, these people do not intend to adopt a no-subsidy CLTS approach seriously. Therefore, if required more than one institutional triggering to bring about the change, as it is essential to convince several people in higher leadership over a period of time.

A similar challenging situation was confronted in 2003–2004 in Indonesia. The Water and Sanitation Programme of the World Bank, East Asia and Pacific Region, Jakarta, introduced CLTS in Indonesia through the WESLIC II project (Water and Sanitation for Low Income Communities). CLTS was introduced in a few selected WESLIC II project districts of East and West Java, Sumatra, East Nusa Tenggara, and West Nusa Tenggara provinces of Indonesia. The outcome of CLTS triggering was fascinating and impressive in all the provinces of Indonesia, where the local communities had instantly decided to stop the practice of open defecation and construct their own toilets with available local resources. Within six months, the success of CLTS spread like wildfire, and the implementation areas of WESLIC II were flooded with ODF villages. For the first time, the managers of WESLIC II witnessed the power of local communities who, constructed toilets with their own money and resources to completely stop the practice of open defecation without waiting for outside help. This transformation of collective hygiene behaviour was such a significant and powerful precedence that the WESLIC II programme managers had to change course and abandon the interest-free, revolving loans for toilet construction to their target communities. For communities those received interest-free loans from the project earlier neither constructed toilets nor repaid the loan. Another important change that emerged from the success of CLTS was the adoption of the CLTS approach with required modifications in the existing programme and its inclusion in the next phase of WESLIC III (PAMSIMAS). When no-subsidy CLTS was creating history in Java, the Asian Development Bank in Manila was at the last stage of finalising its funding plan for PAMSIMAS. The success story of CLTS convinced them to incorporate the community-led initiative as the main component of PAMSIMAS. The islands of success created in the programme areas of WESLIC II (where communities declared their villages free from open defecation with their own initiative) emerged as live demonstration of the power of local community participation. These communities were used as learning laboratories. Though initially not convinced, the senior decision-makers and government officials who visited these communities and saw for themselves the power of CLTS eventually became supporters and promoters of CLTS, which was very useful in transforming the national sanitation policy fairly quickly.

HOW TO BEGIN: WHO WILL BELL THE CAT?

It is important to mention here that the old and traditional mindset that ruled the development sector over the past decades was based on the principle of providing aid to the poor. While the mindset of outsiders paternalism dominated the equation dividing the rules of engagement into *'uppers/providers'* and *'lowers/recipients'* – the in equality creeps in pushing the spirit of participation out of the window. Such a paternalistic approach by the development agencies in the past proved to be less effective globally. Thousands of unused and defunct toilets are seen in the rural landscapes of many developing countries in the world. No one knows how many millions of dollars were wasted to construct toilets for those who were considered to be very poor and not capable of building their own toilets. The reason for large-scale open defecation practice was thought to be the result of poverty, a lack of awareness and knowledge about the dangers of OD, and often unwillingness to change the old and traditional custom of relieving themselves far away from home. With the innovation of CLTS in Bangladesh in 2000[42], it was learned that the earlier notion of outsiders was wrong. In fact, nobody wanted to live in a filthy environment and defecate in the open. The reason for the continued practice of OD was the financial inability of the rural community to construct the expensive toilet models prescribed and advocated by development agencies. In the past, only a couple of toilet models were offered by the front-line extension staff of the government and other development agencies. Mostly, they were Ventilated Improved Pit (VIP) latrines. Masonry SanPlats were provided by some external agencies while, others constructed latrines with both sub structure and super structure free of cost.

Obviously, these toilets were costly and dependent on high external inputs. In early 2000 it is was learnt for the first time in Rajshahi district of Bangladesh, that the cost and model of the toilet were not as important in breaking the faecal oral contamination link as it was equally important to confine the human excreta and arrest the spread of contaminants by other means. The faecal-oral contamination can stop only when there is no excreta in the open and the human faeces

42 Kar, K. and Pasteur, P. (2005) 'Subsidy or self-respect? Community -led Total Sanitation: an update on recent developments', IDS Working Paper 257, Brighton: Institute of Development Studies.

are safely confined. The community of Mosmail village got excited to discover that their own simple toilet design could do the same job and fulfil the purpose. Once a local and low cost alternative design of toilet was invented by the community through my facilitation life became easier for them. Community jumped into action and there was no looking back from there. Hundreds of low-cost designs of toilets emerged from the villages of Bangladesh[43]. In a situation like this, it was difficult to incorporate this powerful learning of collective behaviour change into the national sanitation policy, which was heavily dependent on engineering design and free hardware material supply. It was difficult for the water and sanitation department of the government, mostly dominated by engineers and technologists, to accept this. It was never thought that open defecation could be stopped without external engineering intervention. For the first time ever, CLTS changed the focus from the construction of toilets of particular design to the social element of collective behaviour change in the community. It worked very well when the interventions were made with only triggering without any mention of free or subsidised toilet material supply to the community. The community took their own decision to stop the practice of open defecation, mainly triggered by the fact that they were ingesting each other's faeces so long as open defecation continues and the environment is contaminated with faeces. Behaviour change largely replaced the message of construction of prescribed latrine models as the only intervention. Sharing toilets, pit covers, construction of low cost pit latrines, and many other innovative approaches changed the scenario drastically from one solution to multiple solutions and paved the way for rapid multiplication and spread of CLTS in rural Bangladesh and eventually to other countries in Asia and Africa. The monster of an expensive latrine with an externally prescribed engineering design started losing ground and finally replaced largely in rural areas of Bangladesh and elsewhere removed.

43 Kar, K. 2003, Subsidy or self-respect? Participatory total sanitation in Bangladesh, IDS Working Paper 184, Brighton Sussex BN1 9RE, England.

In some countries, household-level hardware sanitation subsidies are often given to beneficiaries with the plea of helping the poor as a blanket solution. This is often provided to people across regions, nations and states, disregarding the local contexts like levels of poverty, the affordability of new modern toilets, its repair and maintenance, and the availability of hardware sanitary materials in the local market. Mostly all the people, irrespective of their wellbeing status, were given the same material or monetary benefits. Considering the construction of toilets as the only solution to meet sanitation challenges, the most important aspect of sustained hygiene behaviour change was overlooked, leading to poor utilisation of toilets and the continuation of OD. It is important to mention here that in many such situations where people were poor enough to construct latrines, they often spent more money acquiring sophisticated gadgets like mobile phones, motorbikes and other expensive household commodities, etc. Often, clever people in villages portray themselves as poor and eligible to receive government support whenever sanitation subsidies or free distribution of materials are given. This tendency is more pronounced in countries where government decisions are influenced by populist politicians who look at the free supply of goodies to people to win over the voters/ electorates.

In such cases, ongoing programmes supported by donor agencies are generally focused on implementing traditional sanitation approaches like free or subsidised construction of sanitation infrastructure, prescriptions of models, and top-down teaching. These are in fact 'passive participation' or 'participation for material incentives' where local communities are not involved in planning and decision-making. Unlike the CLTS approach, which leads to interactive participation or self-mobilisation, these kinds of participation do not lead to true empowerment of the local communities. Outsiders' subsidy or support poses a challenge to local empowerment. Often, due to vested interests and to have control over the process, the decision-makers continue to implement traditional top-down programmes. Therefore, it might also happen that in the same country, mixed approaches are applied at the same time.

For example, in Madagascar, even after the institutional actors were triggered and all the regions had changed their approach to implementing CLTS, an African lending agency continued to implement a construction-oriented, subsidised sanitation approach in one of the regions of Madagascar. This created confusion, and the progress of sanitation in a particular region was dismal as compared to the other regions.

In some other countries, governments have a powerful presence across different administrative functions, and these are used to channel resources in the name of pro-poor development. Often there exists a hidden agenda of providing money or resources to the poor (below the poverty line) or even to those outside of the eligible category (above the poverty line) to garner their political support. In most cases, this monetary support for sanitation infrastructure and hardware becomes counterproductive for collective behaviour change for sustainable sanitation improvement as the acquisition of toilet an asset scores higher over changing hygiene behaviour. Globally, there are millions of examples where toilets are being used for purposes other than the purpose for which they were built.

The above-mentioned case scenario describes a complex and difficult situation where, in spite of proving its success, the CLTS approach could not be scaled up in a country due to the lack of an enabling environment and supportive national sanitation policy. There are examples of countries where the efficiency of the CLTS approach has been accepted across all levels of the government and non-government sectors. Yet the national and regional policymakers did not officially roll out CLTS for the sustainable benefit of millions in the country. The reasons could be that no one wanted to be responsible for taking the unpopular decision of stopping the free flow of money and material as subsidies to the people. Needless to mention here that the tendency of offering free meals to the electorate is often a popular practise by political leaders in an electoral democracy.

Traditionally, the general tendency of externally induced development intervention is to hide behind the popular notion of helping the poor. As the mindset of the government and donor agencies revolves around the notion of helping the poor with a philanthropic and welfare attitude providing free dole to the community has been ingrained in their mindsets. This is one of the major problems, which derails the focus of igniting collective behaviour change as a sustainable solution to end the practice of OD. However, people with power and authority belonging to higher political and senior administrative level e.g., Chief Ministers of states in India (sanitation is a state subject in India), Regional Governors, Mozambique, Timor-Leste, *Bhupatis* of *Kabupaten* (Chief Administrator of the district) in Indonesia, Chief of Chiefdoms in Zambia and Prefect of provinces in Madagascar etc. It was important to trigger those people at the highest order of the decision-making in a country or region. An effective way to convince them could be through face-to-face interaction between the leaders and ODF communities. Arranging visits by the natural leaders of ODF communities to non-ODF villages to facilitate personal interactions between them could be another way of spreading the success stories of ODF communities.

In India, once the Chief Minister of Haryana and Himachal Pradesh was convinced about the power of local communities in totally eliminating the practice of open defecation, it did not take much time for the state machinery to accept the no-subsidy CLTS approach in sanitation to tackle the crisis of OD and poor sanitation. In order to trigger the Chief Minister and the minister of rural development, it was crucial to inform the top leadership about the fundamental difference between toilet construction and its usage. Widespread non-utilisation of the existing toilets became a major problem, causing the failure of the big programme. Haryana was one of the states with very high toilet coverage, which was more than 86% calculated on the basis of hardware subsidies distributed to individual households. Unfortunately, the percentage of usage of these toilets was only 46% as reported from the field survey data of the government. Therefore, a large number of people were still continuing the practice of open defecation while the construction of individual household toilets continued. The CM also realised that, at the rate at which toilet construction was going on, the state would soon exceed 100% toilet coverage. Unfortunately, more than 50% of the population would still continue to defecate in the open.

Soon after realising the situation, the CM and RD ministers ordered a no-subsidy awareness campaign and to adopt CLTS as the main approach to sanitation. The impact of the CM's order of initiating the no subsidy CLTS approach was immediate in stopping free construction of individual household toilets. The CM also announced a collective community reward for ODF communities. The funding earmarked for household subsidy was used to help the ODF community to climb the sanitation ladder as a post-ODF support. This shift from the provision of *hardware sanitation subsidies* to *collective community rewards* recognised the importance of collective behaviour change and brought the community together to achieve the common goal. This strategy also brought about strong social solidarity, unlike the subsidised approach, which often created divisions within a community. It was the outsiders who often identified the rich and poor according to their criteria, which often differed from the local communities perceptions of rich, medium, and poor.

The above was a strong example where sanitation subsidy was underplayed and community-led initiatives were given the prime focus by the government of Uttar Pradesh, Haryana, Himachal Pradesh, and a few other states in India. It is important to note that these state governments played the subsidy card intelligently. Whereby they shifted the subsidy as a post ODF reward. This way by changing the name and the timing of fund release not only broke the mindset of dependence on external input but also mobilised local resources, zeal and enthusiasm of the community towards achieving a most important milestone in environmental sanitation.

Under these circumstances, CLTS was implemented in some districts of the state. The triggered communities realized the need to stop open defecation and the importance of sustained hygiene behaviour change. Though a major proportion of community members wanted to undertake actions to stop open defecation, they could not stop the practice of OD totally because some members did not have access to toilets due to various reasons and continued to defecate in the open. The triggered communities understood the importance and concept of CLTS, but the alluring nature of the government subsidy continued to act as a hindrance. District-level officials tried to combat the subsidy menace, which further hindered the communities from stopping open defecation.

A two-day workshop on 'Good Practices on SBM-G (Grameen)'

Brainstorming and discussions were held in Lucknow, Uttar Pradesh, in 2016 on the topic of achieving an ODF state. District officials from 18 selected districts of the state of Uttar Pradesh shared their experiences of triggered communities. These district officials had attempted to implement the CLTS approach actively within the realms of a policy that provided individual household hardware subsidies. The workshop showcased the enormous amount of effort and resources that were being invested by the district officials in the implementation of the CLTS approach in order to combat household hardware subsidy-driven sanitation efforts. These officials understood how the CLTS approach encouraged the communities towards self-mobilisation and combating the unhealthy practice of open defecation.

Some enthusiastic officials from the selected few districts had utilised the CLTS tools and techniques to ignite self-mobilisation and a sense of social solidarity amongst the triggered community members, which led to collective local action. For example, in Bijnor district of Uttar Pradesh, the Chief Development Officer (CDO) introduced an innovative term for toilets. The toilet was named an 'Izzat Ghar' in Hindi, which meant 'a place of dignity', thus broadening the scope of safe sanitation to values of self-respect and dignity. The focus was shifted from the construction of toilets to generating sustainable collective behaviour change. The communities were empowered, and various supervision committees were formed to monitor and fast-track the progress towards achieving ODF status. There was a shift from individual household hardware subsidies to community rewards, which made each community responsible for their ODF priorities and targets.

The triggered communities undertook collective actions to identify the community members who continued to practice OD and started helping them with the necessary support to start sharing neighbours/relatives toilets and gradually builds their own.

In a few villages in Bijnor district, once all the households constructed their own toilets, the community collectively decided to combine the total individual household subsidy amount earmarked for the village and utilise the funds to improve roads, build water points, construct schools, etc. Such innovative solutions led to the emergence of natural leaders, who took further steps to fast-track the progress of sanitation.

These examples showcased the negative impact of hardware subsidies on the progress of sustainable sanitation. It was clearly understood and duly recognised by the local officials. In this case, subsidy was underplayed and importance was given to the power of community-led initiatives and mechanisms to involve the entire community. However, it is crucial to have a supportive policy environment to scale up these innovative solutions across the state or the entire nation. This change is only possible if the state or the nation's focus is on achieving ODF communities across the country rather than on the construction of toilets alone. In other words, emergence of ODF communities is the desired outcome of the investment in sanitation by the government/ NGOs and other development agencies. Often we miss the outcome and get entangled with the integrities of output. The driving force behind participation is enthusiasm[44]. Therefore, efforts to achieve ODF status by local communities should be appreciated and rewarded in various forms that enlightens and further encourages their enthusiasm.

44 Bunch. R, 1995 World Neighbors, Oklahoma City, Okla.

References

1. Kamal Kar and Robert Chambers, *Handbook on Community-Led Total Sanitation*. Plan UK, 2008 and Venkataramanan, Vidya, et al. "Community-Led Total Sanitation: A Mixed-Methods Systematic Review of Evidence and Its Quality." *Environmental Health Perspectives*, vol. 126, no. 2, 2018, doi:10.1289/ehp1965.
2. Kamal Kar, *Scaling-Up CLTS*, 2018.
3. UNICEF/WHO/World Bank Joint Child Malnutrition Estimates: Stunting (National and Disaggregated). UNICEF and Water Supply and Sanitation in Niger. Water and Sanitation Program, www.wsp.org/sites/wsp/files/publications/CSO-Niger.pdf.
4. Kar K. (2018) *Scaling-Up Community Led Total Sanitation: From Village to Nation*, Rugby, UK: Practical Action Publishing <http://dx.doi.org/10.3362/9781780449753
5. Kar K. (2018) *Scaling-Up Community Led Total Sanitation: From Village to Nation*, Rugby, UK: Practical Action Publishing <http://dx.doi.org/10.3362/9781780449753
6. Amy Pickering, Amy, et al, "Effect of a Community-Led Sanitation Intervention on Child Diarrhoea and Child Growth in Rural Mali: A Cluster-Randomised Controlled Trial." *The Lancet Global Health*, vol. 3, Nov. 2015, 701–711., www.thelancet.com/action/showPdf?pii=S2214-109X(15)00144-8.
7. Kar K. (2018) *Scaling-Up Community Led Total Sanitation: From Village to Nation*, Rugby, UK: Practical Action Publishing <http://dx.doi.org/10.3362/9781780449753.
8. Lawrence, J. Joseph, et al. "Beliefs, Behaviours, and Perceptions of Community-Led Total Sanitation and Their Relation to Improved Sanitation in Rural Zambia." *The American Journal of Tropical Medicine and Hygiene*, vol. 94, no. 3, 2016, 553–562., doi:10.4269/ajtmh.15-0335.
9. Kar K. (2018) *Scaling-Up Community Led Total Sanitation: From Village to Nation*, Rugby, UK: Practical Action Publishing <http://dx.doi.org/10.3362/9781780449753.
10. https://www.cedlas.econo.unlp.edu.ar/wp/wp-content/uploads/mali-clts-impact-evaluation-2014.pdf
11. Pretty, J. (1995) Participatory learning for sustainable agriculture, World Development, 23 (8), 1247–1263.
12. https://www.who.int/publications/i/item/9789240006416

13. https://jogh.org/documents/issue201802/jogh-08-020309.pdf
14. Intersector Coordination Group. Situation Update: Rohingya Refugee Crisis Cox's Bazar. Intersector Coordination Group; 2018.
15. Watch HR. World Report 2017. Available: http://www.hrw.org/world-report/2017. Accessed: 30 October 2017.
16. United Nations Children's Fund. Outcast and Desperate: Rohingya refugee children face a perilous Future. New York: UNICEF; 2017
17. United Nations High Commissioner for Refugees. Operational Update-Bangladesh. Geneva: UNHCR; 2017.
18. United Nations Children's Fund. Bangladesh Humanitarian Situation report-10 (Rohingya Influx). New York: UNICEF; 2017
19. World Health Organization. Weekly Situation Report. Bangladesh: WHO; 2018.
20. United Nations High Commissioner for Refugee. Disease threatens refugees in Bangladesh in unplanned sites. Geneva: UNHCR; 2017
21. Women UN. Gender Brief on Rohingya Refugee Crisis Response in Bangladesh. New York: UN Women; 2017.
22. United Nations Children's Fund. Bangladesh Humanitarian Situation report-8 (Rohingya Influx). New York: UNICEF; 2017.
23. "Populations disproportionally affected by climate change" was not defined in the GLAAS 2021/2022 country survey, as different countries have different definitions of these populations.
24. Water, sanitation, hygiene and health: a primer for health professionals. Geneva: World Health Organization; 2019 (https:// apps.who.int/iris/handle/10665/330100, accessed 21 October 2022)
25. The facilitators should make it a point to involve institutions beyond ministries/ government departments responsible for WASH, such as finance, home, and internal affairs (what percentage of national sanitation budget allocated for sanitation); health (often there is a great imbalance in the investment on curative measures and very little on prophylactic/preventive measures), education (schools, institutional WASH, involving students as agents of change), and tourism.
26. Such as drawing the map which will be used for the triggering exercise—this is described in detail in the Institutional Triggering section.
27. Chambers, Robert, 1932-.Participatory workshops: a sourcebook of 21 sets of ideas and activities / Robert Chambers.
28. Kar, Kamal (2010) 'Facilitating "Hands-On" Training: Workshops for Community-Led Total Sanitation. A Trainers' Training Guide", WSSCC, Geneva.

29. Kar, K and Pasteur, P. (2005) 'Subsidy or self-respect? Community- Led Total Sanitation: an update on recent developments', IDS Working Paper 257, Brighton: Institute of Development Studies.

30. https://www.statista.com/statistics/510498/total-population-of-eritrea/.

31. Kar, Kamal with Robert Chambers (2008) Handbook on Community-Led Total Sanitation, Brighton London: Institute of Development Studies and Plan UK

32. Kar, Kamal with Robert Chambers (2008) Handbook on Community-Led Total Sanitation, Brighton London: Institute of Development Studies and Plan UK

33. Pretty, J. (1995) Participatory learning for sustainable agriculture, World Development, 23 (8), 1247–1263.

34. Kar, K. and Pasteur, P. (2005) 'Subsidy or self-respect? Community -led Total Sanitation: an update on recent developments', IDS Working Paper 257, Brighton: Institute of Development Studies.

35. Kar, K. 2003, Subsidy or self-respect? Participatory total sanitation in Bangladesh, IDS Working Paper 184, Brighton Sussex BN1 9RE, England.

36. Bunch. R, 1995 World Neighbors, Oklahoma City, Okla.

About the Author

Kamal Kar is an international development specialist in the sphere of natural resources, management, agriculture, and rural development with decades of experience working in over 45 countries in Asia, Africa, and Latin America. He has successfully pioneered a number of innovative approaches in natural resource management by local communities, including nomadic herders, and appropriate low-cost technologies in farming. He has also worked in the areas of urban poverty, slum improvement, and local governance in India, Mongolia, Bangladesh, and Cambodia.

As a social entrepreneur, Kar has taken on the challenge of ending open defecation in the developing world. He pioneered the Community-Led Total Sanitation (CLTS) approach 1999-2000 in Bangladesh, then introduced it to other countries in Asia, including India, Indonesia, Cambodia, and Pakistan, before taking the approach to Eastern and Southern Africa in 2006 and to West Africa in 2007. This methodology has a no-subsidy policy and is deeply embedded in community empowerment and mobilization. The approach has transformed global development thinking on open defecation by departing from a focus on toilet construction to the process of collective behavior change. CLTS has spread over 73 countries across the continents of Asia, Africa, and Latin America where more than 50 million people are living in an open defecation free (ODF) environment. The approach has been mainstreamed in the sanitation policies of over 30 countries in these regions. Kar has played a crucial role in the spread of CLTS at the global scale through his capacity building, policy advocacy, and process support efforts to various national governments and international organizations, including DFID, GIZ, Asian Development Bank, World Bank, UNICEF,

WSSCC, Irish Aid, WHO, DFAT, Plan International, WaterAid, SNV, World Vision, and CARE among others.

Kar initiated the Sost Gulicha (three stone stove) Free in five villages of Gamo zone of Ethiopia in the year 2018 which is now being scaled up by many NGOs and government to become a movement in rural Ethiopia. This approach is called as Community Led Total Stove (CLT-S) approach.

Kar is the principal author of the seminal book on CLTS, *Handbook on Community-Led Total Sanitation (2008),* which has been translated into more than 16 languages. He is also the author of the first inclusive training manual on CLTS, entitled *Facilitating 'Hands-on' Training Workshop for Community-Led Total Sanitation: A Trainers' Training Guide,* which was published in 2010. In addition, he has documented his experience in *Promising Pathways: Innovations and Best Practice in CLTS at scale in Madagascar (2014), CLTS Rapid Appraisal Protocol (CRAP)* (August 2017), a joint publication by CLTS Foundation and UNICEF ESARO, and in other practice and strategy papers. He is also the author of the book *Scaling-up Community-Led Total Sanitation from Village to Nation* published in 2019 which provides with detailed instructions on how to facilitate CLTS in a village and how to scale up and institutionalize the CLTS approach at regional and national level.

Kar holds the esteemed position of Honorary Associate at the Institute of Development Studies, University of Sussex, UK and is an Adjunct Faculty at the Institute of Water Policy of Lee Kuan Yew School of Public Policy at the National University of Singapore. The prestigious *Foreign Policy* magazine of Washington, DC recognized Kar as one of the Top Hundred Global Thinkers of the World in 2010. The Asian Development Bank declared Kar the Water Champion of 2011. For his prolific work in the sanitation sector spanning many continents, governments, and communities, Kar also received the revered Sarphati Sanitation Lifetime Achievement Award in 2015 from World Waternet, Netherlands Water Partnership (NWP) and Aqua for All. Kar was honoured with the prestigious Safaigiri Award in association with the India Today Group for creating an Open Defecation Free blueprint for the World Global Mission in 2019. Among other awards, Kar was the recipient of the prestigious Global Leader in Humanitarian Service Award presented by Lions International in 2013. He has also been feted by various national governments, including Mongolia, Pakistan, Indonesia, Bangladesh, Nepal, Kenya, and other countries in Asia and Africa, for his service.

www.ingramcontent.com/pod-product-compliance
Lightning Source LLC
LaVergne TN
LVHW041202150826
845673LV00001B/261

* 9 7 9 8 8 9 0 2 6 4 7 4 9 *